GROWING PLANTS FROM SEED

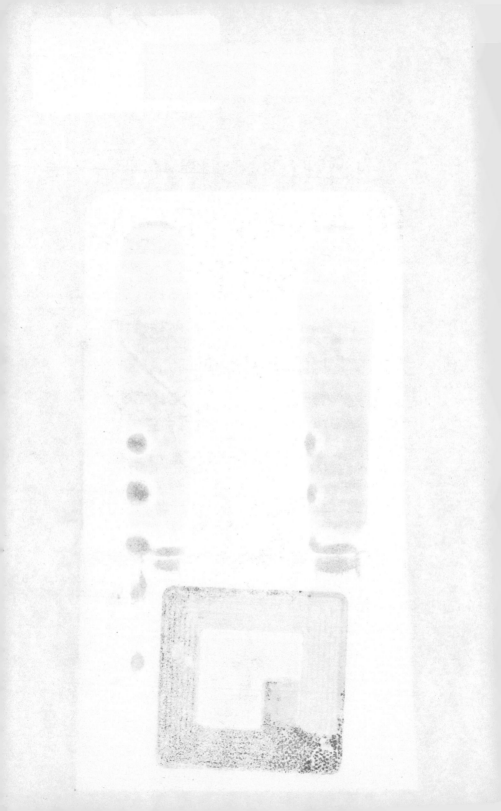

"GROWING PLANTS FROM SEED"

John Kelly

WARD LOCK

First published in the UK 1996

by Ward Lock, Wellington House, 125 Strand
London WC2R 0BB

A Cassell Imprint

Text copyright © John Kelly 1996

Distributed in the United States by Sterling Publishing Co., Inc.
387 Park Avenue South, New York, NY 10016-8810

A British Library Cataloguing in Publication Data block for this book may be obtained from the British Library

ISBN 0-7063-7470-3

Typeset by York House Typographic Ltd
Printed and bound in Great Britain by Biddles Ltd

CONTENTS

FOREWORD

by *Janie Pirie*
Public Relations Manager,
Thompson & Morgan (UK) Ltd

Growing young plants from seed is one of the most satisfying and enjoyable pastimes you are likely to encounter. Certainly I find no greater reward in gardening than seeing fresh, bright green leaves, full of promise for the future, emerging from the dark compost.

Notwithstanding the delight that accompanies success – and you will succeed with most seeds – growing from seed can be a tricky business. Some seeds are fitted by nature with mechanisms that make them cautious about leaving the safety of the seed coat and chancing the world outside, while others are easy to germinate but difficult to rear. There are seeds that you may find expensive, such as the F_1 hybrids, but if you take time and care you will be rewarded with enough plants for yourself and perhaps to give away to others, at a fraction of the price you would have to pay to purchase them ready grown.

The firm of Thompson & Morgan was established in 1855 and its success in the industry has been achieved through a long line of highly experienced horticulturists who have made our name synonymous with quality and reliability. We are on record as suppliers of seed to Charles Darwin and Claude Monet and have been known for many decades as suppliers of seed of the more rare and interesting plants from around the world. With a little care and the advice you will find in the pages of this book you will find your range of plants growing ever wider.

While we pride ourselves on giving gardeners precise instructions on the backs of all our seed packets, there is never enough room to go into fine detail and we are delighted that John Kelly has written this comprehensive and eminently readable book. We are even more delighted to be associated with its publication. John has more than 30 years experience as a nurseryman and gardener, during which he raised countless batches of seed of everything from peas to passionflowers and gained considerable understanding of the problems encountered by the gardening public. This book is written for all gardeners, from novices to the most experienced, and is packed full of helpful tips and information.

My colleagues and I are quite certain that this book will be of the greatest service to seed-growers everywhere. There will certainly be a place for it in my greenhouse, not least because of my confidence in the author's horticultural soundness.

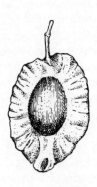

SEEDS AND GERMINATION

*Or what are seeds and why do
they 'come up'?*

WHAT IS A SEED?

'What is a seed?' sounds like a fairly silly question. Everyone knows what a seed is, surely. And yet do we really? When you stop to think about it (which hardly anyone does), the answer comes out as something like 'Well, you know, a *seed*'.

Most gardeners see a seed as a small, usually hard thing mainly between the size of a conker (horse chestnut) and a grain of pepper. It may have attached to it some form of transport assistance such as a parachute (dandelion), a propeller (sycamore) or a life-jacket (coconut) and it is dry to the touch. You put it in the soil or specially prepared compost and hope for the best. Some seeds will come up every time, others will produce a few seedlings if you are lucky, while still more refuse to do anything at all.

If you really understand seeds and above all know precisely what a seed is, your chances of getting good results with a very wide range of seeds – trees, shrubs, herbaceous perennials, defiant bulbs, tricky alpines and truculent tropicals – are greatly increased. This is why I have asked, 'What is a seed?'. The next thing is to provide the answer.

Superman may seem to have nothing whatever to do with the germination of seeds, but in fact his early history as depicted in the film has a great deal to tell us. Do you remember that, when his home planet was collapsing, his parents put the baby Superman in a space capsule and fired him out into the cosmos to find

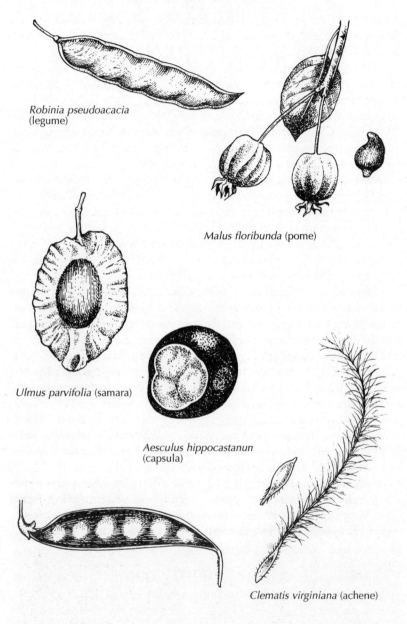

Robinia pseudoacacia
(legume)

Malus floribunda (pome)

Ulmus parvifolia (samara)

Aesculus hippocastanun
(capsula)

Clematis virginiana (achene)

A selection of fruits. Botanically, a fruit is the ovary of a flower and seed or seeds it contains.

somewhere to survive? The capsule eventually landed in an Indiana cornfield, it opened, and Glenn Ford found he had a brand new foster-son.

The capsule opened because there was an atmosphere and gravity that suited the baby's physical make-up. There was oxygen, water, good light and a comfortable temperature. These factors triggered the locks of the capsule, which then split open to reveal the young Clark Kent within and allow him to be taken out and nurtured until he could leap tall buildings at a single bound and make a complete hash of courting Lois Lane.

A seed works in a similar way. Sometimes it waits quite a long time – perhaps a whole year or even two – to make absolutely certain that it has arrived in a safe and suitable place, but in general it will germinate if its four locks – each in turn sensitive to water, oxygen, light and temperature – are persuaded to open. All four must be opened; if three conditions are satisfactory but the fourth is not, then the seed will not germinate.

Therefore to answer the question 'What is a seed?' it is legitimate to reply that a seed is a liferaft launched by the parent plant in the hope that it will eventually find itself in a congenial place in which its embryo may develop, emerge and grow to maturity in order to produce yet more seed and thus perpetuate the species. If you think nature exists with anything other in mind than keeping each species going, you are romantic or religious but not very scientific. The best approach for gardeners is to be romantic and never lose the joy of seeing seedlings emerge, to be religious enough to wonder at the order of the natural world, and to be sufficiently scientific to see the basic, fairly harsh truths that lie behind the way nature really works.

If you do take it on board that the main impetus behind the life force is to perpetuate the species it will help your growing from seed enormously, as it will make an optimist of you and prevent your plunging into resentment at the seeds when they seem

Essentials for germination — the four locks

Before any seed can germinate it requires exposure to oxygen, water, the right level of light and the right temperature.

obstinately to refuse to come up. Some gardeners even get themselves into a state in which mumbo-jumbo, incantations and spells govern their thoughts on seed-raising. Have you ever lifted the lid of the frame or propagator and muttered, 'Come on, you b*****s, germinate!'? Well, if you have, don't feel alone, but at the same time allow yourself to feel confident that such things are behind you as your understanding of seed grows and your frustration recedes.

In a seed lies the fierce force of life. Plants of course have no will, no aspirations or intentions, nor even any instincts. They are best thought of as bags of living chemical soup. On the other hand, within them is a drive stronger than any other on our planet: that to survive. Seeds have evolved to survive, not to sulk, and if you give them the chance they *will* come up. Unless a seed is dead or unfilled (contains no embryo) when you obtain it, it will only fail to germinate because you have not provided the right conditions.

WHAT DO SEEDS NEED?

The conditions that persuade a seed to germinate are bound up with the four locking mechanisms and must provide the keys. Of the four – water, oxygen, light and temperature – the one that seems most obvious is water.

WATER

Everyone knows you have to water seeds to get them started. A seed, however, will not be unlocked by one watering. If it were, it would be vulnerable to coming to life in an area far too dry for it but with the occasional heavy shower. It needs to 'know' that there is a reasonably constant supply of moisture and that it won't be killed by drought in its first few days or weeks of life and before it can send roots down to deep layers where there is likely to be long-term moisture.

Germination starts when water penetrates the seed coat and initiates chemical changes within the tissues inside. Once begun, these changes cannot be reversed, and if the supply of water ceases and the process is unable to continue, the seed simply dies. Thus, if you water your newly sown seeds and then let them dry out, there is a strong chance that you will convert a pot of healthy, eager seeds into dead ones.

You are much more likely to kill the seeds by letting them dry out after a few waterings than after just one or two. This is because the seed coat has to be softened first and it leads to the delay the plant needs in nature before it is safe to start the germination process. It is all too easy to be really careful at first and then, as time goes on and nothing comes up, to become careless and allow dry conditions to develop. It is likely that this is just precisely the time when you should be most watchful, as the seed will be at its most confident about its surroundings.

I won't apologize for discussing seeds in terms of their 'knowing', 'anticipating', 'feeling confident' and so on. They do nothing of the sort, of course, but such notions do make it much easier to describe their reactions. A botanist friend once took me to task for writing such things and then, when I admired his dog, told me, 'Oh yes! And he understands every word you say, you know'.

Seeds just about double their size in the process of taking up enough water to start germinating. The seed coats stretch slightly, and they split at this stage, allowing more water and much more oxygen to come into contact with the contents and assist the processes of growth.

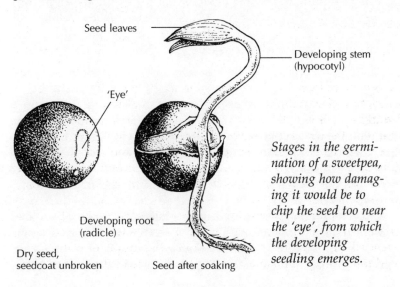

Seed leaves

Developing stem (hypocotyl)

'Eye'

Developing root (radicle)

Dry seed, seedcoat unbroken

Seed after soaking

Stages in the germination of a sweetpea, showing how damaging it would be to chip the seed too near the 'eye', from which the developing seedling emerges.

OXYGEN

Oxygen is the second of the four vital keys to unlocking the seed. One might just as well call it air, as that is the main form in which oxygen reaches a seed. If you sow seeds on a sticky compost or a clay soil and apply too much water that then lies about on or near the surface, the water will take up the space that air could occupy. The oxygen dissolved in the water will help for a short while, but the seed will fail to germinate. It will rot very quickly as the water will soften the seed coat and start the chemical changes, but in the wet, airless conditions fungi will enter and kill the seed very quickly.

Oxygen is vital to the chemical changes that go on inside a seed as it germinates. These chiefly involve the changing of food storage substances such as starches into sugars and proteins, then into smaller units called amino-acids. These are then used to build up the tissues of the emerging plant. The process is called respiration and, as in human beings, it cannot take place without oxygen.

A well-drained compost will go a long way to keeping a fresh, oxygen-rich, airy atmosphere round the seeds. However, if it is too gravelly or sandy it will not retain enough moisture. Over-frequent watering will drive out the air for too much of the time; watering too seldom will allow in plenty of air but not enough moisture.

It is beginning to become evident that providing the right conditions is a matter of balance. This is, however, true of almost all natural systems. Once we understand the importance of balance, we are well along the road to true sympathy with plant life and eventually with all of nature.

LIGHT

Light is slightly less simple in its effects on seeds. Generally speaking, though, it is possible to say that a seed needs to know that it is near the surface of the soil and not too far down for its shoot to reach the sun and air. All a seed can tell is dark and light – if it is a few centimetres down it might as well be several metres. Darkness can have two effects – the seed passes beyond its natural life and dies, or it goes dormant and lives for possibly thousands of years.

A few seeds need complete darkness to germinate, but they are very few. Most need some light. Seeds of plants that in nature live

(a) *This frame is in full sun but is shaded with fine mesh netting. Most seeds will germinate as long as there is daily attention to watering;*

(b) *The frame has been placed with its back to some deciduous shrubs. Depending on the direction the frame faces, it may be shaded with mesh (south- or west-facing) or left unshaded (north- or east-facing), as the branches will provide light shade;*

(c) *You should never site a frame near evergreen shrubs or trees as the constant shade means that most seeds will not germinate.*

In both (b) and (c) you will find green algae on the surface of the glass becoming a nuisance.

on the floor of deciduous forest are often very small and when they are sown into compost need to be on its surface so that they have maximum light. This is because they then 'know' that the leaves have not yet arrived above them and that it is a good time to make their early growth in the maximum light. If they are in the relative dark – as they are when covered by even only a thin layer of compost – they will fail to come up because they 'think' they will be shaded by the tree canopy and will have inadequate light and moisture during the time it takes for their roots to become established. Thus you will tend to find yourself advised to sow such seed as *Primula* and *Meconopsis* on the surface of the compost.

In fact, all very fine seed is best sown on the surface, as its diameter is liable to be minute in comparison with the thinnest covering layer of compost you can contrive. Where a larger seed would still receive plenty of light, a tiny one may well imagine itself well underground, impossibly shaded by leaves, or under a pile of leaf litter.

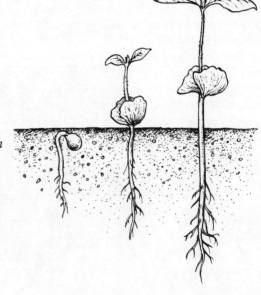

Stages in germination of a plant with two seed leaves. Seeds of flowering plants have either one seed leaf (for example the grass, lily, crocus, and iris families) or, as in most other plants, two.

Interestingly, many sun-loving plants avoid germinating in shade by being sensitive to the amount of red in daylight. Under trees, there is less red as it is absorbed by the green pigment in the leaves. Forest-floor plants have much the same sensitivity and will remain dormant if the red wavelengths are cut down. Obviously, an overall reduction of daylight involves a reduction of the red wavelengths too, but to put your unshaded seed frame where its light passes through leaves will give you worse overall results than if it is facing the sun but lightly shaded with fine, white or grey muslin or scrim.

TEMPERATURE

Every chemical process has a temperature range within which it can take place. If the temperature falls outside that range, the reaction does not happen. In plants the range is quite narrow. If a seed is too cold or too hot it will not germinate and some seeds have very fine limits to the warmth they will tolerate, while others need much higher temperatures before they will even 'think' about germinating.

Cold may be thought of as a universal inhibitor of seed germination once the temperature falls to 5°C (41°F). Between this and freezing point, water expands. It does not do so at a lower temperature. At this critical temperature, plant growth ceases and germination cannot occur.

In general, you can say that warmth encourages germination but that too much warmth discourages it. This is really quite logical, as you would expect the plant to need to 'know' that spring had arrived but not yet summer. This, however, applies only to plants from parts of the world with well-marked seasons. Tropical seeds need to feel only that they are still in the tropics – even if they are not.

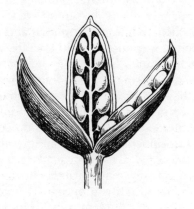

2

SEEDS AND DELAYED GERMINATION

Or why do some seeds not 'come up'?

FAILURE TO GERMINATE

Supposing you have apparently done everything right and seem to have provided the ideal conditions for unlocking the seeds – and they still do not germinate: what then? There is a good supply of water, the soil or compost is well drained, the light is just right and the temperature spot on. What more can one do?

The seeds in the batch may be dead. You must consider this. Seeds are alive when they leave the plant but can be killed in storage or in transit. This is unlikely to occur when the seed is supplied by a reputable seed house such as Thompson & Morgan or another well-known company but may well happen with seed from other sources, including your own garden.

Heat and damp are the two big killers, and we shall look at these factors and how to avoid them more closely in a later chapter. Another consideration is what is termed the viability of a seed.

SEED VIABILITY

Seeds of different kinds have differing life-spans. In a cool, dry place a seed will live longer than in a warm, damp one, but even so its potential life (viability) may be measured in days or in thousands of years. Poppy seeds may germinate 1,000 years after being buried by the plough, while those of a Himalayan primula may have but a few weeks to live after being shed by their parent. The inherent dryness of a seed has a good deal to do with its longevity. The driest seeds contain less than 2 per cent water by weight, compared to the 95 per cent in a mature herbaceous plant. In general, the drier the seed, the longer it will live. Seeds with high moisture content, such as oaks, will not live long before shrivelling and must be sown straight away. Curiously enough, black oaks, which make up one of the two divisions of the oak genus (*Quercus*), will then wait until the following spring before germinating, while the white oaks will germinate almost immediately. If you try to store acorns for sowing in spring, they will fail.

Sometimes – but this happens quite rarely – you will find yourself with seed that refuses to germinate because it is 'unfilled'. This means that each seed is devoid of an embryo. It is difficult to spot and something we just have to put up with. Examples are verbenas (60–65 per cent unfilled) and rosemary (55 per cent unfilled). However, in more decades of seed-raising than I care to remember, I can recall only two 100 percent unfilled examples – *Olearia macrodonta* (a New Zealand daisy bush) and *Telopea truncata*, the Tasmanian waratah. If a batch of seed fails to come up, it is far more likely to be due to some other factor rather than the lack of embryos.

DORMANCY

The chief reason for failure is a phenomenon called dormancy. In fact, it is a blanket term for all sorts of mechanisms that delay germination but, as in everything in nature, there is a reason for it.

INNATE DORMANCY

The great majority of seeds – and this includes most annuals – are dormant early in their lives, when they are first shed or first harvested. This is a way of ensuring that the seeds have time to get away from the parents and colonize other areas; those that fall straight to the ground will be delayed, while those that travel will

Why do some seeds fail to germinate?

◆ Is the seed viable?
◆ Is it dormant?
◆ Is it the right season?
◆ Does the seed coat need to break?
◆ Is the seed too cold, too hot, too wet, too dry?

germinate soon after landing. This is called innate dormancy and prevents seeds from germinating where the environment is unsuitable. With annuals and many sun-lovers, they will not germinate until they have experienced good light and a period during which the temperatures go up and down. Without them they are registering neither daylight nor the change in temperature between night and day, and as far as they are concerned they might well be some distance below ground.

THE NEED FOR 'AFTER-RIPENING'

For some seeds a period is needed during which a process called 'after-ripening' takes place. This in effect means that the seed is shed before it is fully mature and that maturity takes place over different intervals of time. The purpose of this is to give the seed the best chance of germination in good conditions by spreading its readiness to germinate over a period of weeks, months, or even sometimes years. *Amelanchier lamarckii*, the well-known snowy mespilus, demonstrates after-ripening (sometimes called differential dormancy) but develops the tendency more strongly after a short period. Thus you will get very good results if you sow it in autumn but the following spring you will obtain just a few seedlings and more will appear at intervals thereafter. If some seeds – notably annuals – are given a period of dry storage after they are harvested, it has the effect of after-ripening, and this is one of the reasons why your seeds of annuals germinate so reliably in spring. The period of cool, dry storage given by the seed company before the seeds are sent out allows after-ripening to be complete and the seeds to be fully ready to germinate as soon as you give them the right conditions.

THE NEED FOR THE RIGHT SEASON

Another kind of innate dormancy is demonstrated by seeds that will not germinate until they are 'satisfied' that certain seasons have passed and that the right one has arrived. Many plants from cool or cold countries are at a disadvantage if they come up during autumn or winter, and have a mechanism that tells them that winter is safely over and gone. They need to experience several weeks in a moist state while the temperature is between 2 and 10°C (36–50°F) and then a spell when it is warmer. Chemical changes take place in the seed during this time and only when they are complete will the growth process begin.

THE SEED COAT AS A CAUSE OF DORMANCY

With other seeds, the seed coat is so dry and hard that it takes a long time for it to break down and allow water to come into contact with the contents. The seed coat may also contain subtances that inhibit germination and will continue to do so until washed out by a prolonged period of moisture – rain in nature. A badly drained compost that stays moist and does not need fairly frequent watering is death to seeds such as this but, on the other hand, the provision of a good compost is unlikely to be enough on its own to overcome the dormancy.

Some scientists use the word 'quiescence' to describe this kind of delay mechanism but it is just as much a case of genuine innate dormancy as any other. It should be contrasted not with them but with acquired or induced dormancy.

ACQUIRED OR INDUCED DORMANCY

Acquired dormancy is usually to be laid at our door rather than that of nature. It occurs when we do something to switch a seed from readiness to reluctance. With many members of the buttercup family, such as *Ranunculus* and *Clematis*, germination will proceed happily if the seed is sown as soon as it is ripe. If sowing is delayed, the seed goes profoundly dormant and will not germinate even in the following spring. Many primulas go dormant if the temperature approaches 21°C (70°F), and lettuces become more demanding in their light requirements as temperatures rise above this figure. In the last two cases, it is a defence against germinating in the summer which would leave the plants with no chance of flowering and setting seed before winter.

DOUBLE DORMANCY

A few plants are doubly dormant. Peonies, for example, require a period of alternating cool temperatures, followed by a warm spell, after which they will produce a radicle (the very young root produced by a seed). Only after a further series of alternating temperatures will a shoot arise. One shudders to think of the bushels of peony seed that have been thrown away when they were in fact perfectly happy doing their own toe-in-the-water thing.

HOW TO DEAL WITH DORMANCY

The idea that nature furnishes seeds with survival mechanisms that are linked to the arrival at a safe place, not just for germination, but for the production of the next generation of seeds, is central to this book and central, I believe, to gardeners' greater understanding of seeds in general.

So, how on earth are you to know which seed does what and when? What a complicated, vexatious business this all is and why in heaven's name should anyone read any further?

Apart from the advice given in this chapter, the lists in Chapters 13, 14 and 15 will tell you a great deal about plants with special requirements. Meanwhile, however, you will be glad to know that for the patient gardener there is a method of proceeding that covers the great majority of cases when it comes to seeds of plants for the open garden – as opposed to greenhouse and house plants and half-hardy annuals which, being for the most part tropical, are in a different order of things.

USING A COLD FRAME

If you sow every batch of hardy seed just as soon it comes into your hands, and put the pots or trays in a cold frame and keep them watered and weed-free, almost everything will eventually germinate. The exceptions will be seeds of plants from warmer climates that are at the margins of hardiness, but even some of these will come up in time. The frame should be in a light position – but not where it gets too hot – and you should open the lights (i.e. the cover) slightly in warm weather. It is much better in fact if you have two frames, as you can move pots from one to the other as they germinate, keeping the second frame a little open to allow air to circulate, while the first remains closed except when it is very warm. More information about sowing and the use of frames is given in Chapter 6.

Some possible drawbacks and some great rewards

The only thing about this system is that you will need plenty of frame space and a long fuse on your patience. You may become convinced that you are wasting your time when a year, two, or even three pass by without a sign of a green shoot. But I cannot describe to you adequately the joy that you will feel when your patience is rewarded. I have never forgotten coming one day upon a luxuriant germination in a half-forgotten tray of *Iris innominata*, a lovely little plant from the western coast of the USA, which I had sown three and a half years previously. The seedlings were planted out and eventually became a drift of neat plants with grassy leaves and maytime flowers of a lovely tan-yellow, swirling about the feet of small rhododendrons and camellias.

It is an advantage to have two cold frames: one (here shown on the left) for germination; the other for hardening off germinated seedlings. The second frame can be kept open with a block of wood or a stay, but should be closed at night while it still contains very young seedlings or when low temperatures are likely.

It is always better to hang tools up and put pots, boxes, trays and other items on shelves, rather than on the floor. The neatest pile of equipment has nooks and crannies which can harbour slugs, woodlice and other pests.

Many very fine gardeners confine their seed-sowing – apart, as I have said, from hot-country plants – to the frames-and-patience system. The trouble with it, however, is that accidents happen. As time passes it is all too easy to allow drying to take place, and as we have seen, that is usually fatal once the seeds have already taken up water. Seeds can remain dormant in what is called the fully imbibed state for a very long time indeed, but if they dry out they are finished. Your holidays, illness, distraction, a sudden hot spell – all these and more can upset the system. It is heartbreaking to find a litter of tiny green bits where slugs have breakfasted on the newly emerged seedlings of a sowing made two years ago, and sad indeed to find the compost and seeds in a pot churned to a foul mess by the earthworm that has got in through a drainage hole.

Nevertheless, for what I suppose to be a majority of gardeners, a couple of frames is about it. Lack of space, finance or inclination leads many of us to do without a greenhouse. Yet there are other things we can do to obtain even better results than the most meticulous seed-watcher.

OPENING THE 'LOCKS' IN THE RIGHT SEQUENCE

I cannot leave the subject of dormancy without mentioning that, after all I have said, I believe it might be a concept that gets in the way of our proper understanding of seeds. The 'four locks' way of looking at germination is a simple one, perhaps even simplistic, and germination is in fact dependent on the provision of air, water, light and the right temperature within a time frame programmed into the seed. During this time frame it may be necessary for the four locks to be opened more than once – or they may in some way be double locks. They may need to occur first out of synchrony with one another and then simultaneously at a later date.

In other words, what we take for 'dormancy' can in fact be seen simply as the seed waiting for the right conditions for safe germination – no different in principle from any other seed. Is a seed of the giant double coconut of the Seychelles dormant while floating along on the surface of the ocean, or merely waiting until it is cast ashore and the conditions are right for it to germinate?

DEALING WITH DORMANCY
NATURE'S WAY AND THE GARDENER'S WAY

Now we should consider once more the difference between our expectations as gardeners and those of nature. We want to maximize germination to the extent of inducing *all* the seeds to come up. Nature allows for those that fall by the wayside and those that fall on stony ground. She also sees fit to give some seeds of a species more resistance to seemingly favourable conditions than others, rather like those granules of medicinal drugs put within the same capsule but given different thicknesses of coatings in order to allow slow release. What is important to nature is not the number of seeds that germinate but the height of the chances that there will be further generations of seeds. If it is more or less a certainty that out of a set of 1,000 seeds 50 are virtually certain to grow to be

---

The four locks and the seed's own time frame

◆ Some locks need to be 'opened' more than once
◆ The locks may have to open in a specific order
◆ Some locks may have to open simultaneously

---

seed-bearers themselves, the species is secure and is not necessarily made more so if 500 germinate.

If we sow a batch of seed in late winter and just a few come up, we tend to treat the species as one whose seeds are dormant. In fact, we should perhaps view it as one that hedges its bets, allowing some seedlings to face a chancy future, followed by others with greater and greater opportunities for security as time passes. We refer to the seed of *Campanula morettiana*, an alpine from high ledges in the Dolomites, as dormant for two years at least, when in fact it needs to have its locks triggered twice – once to tell it that the conditions for germination do in fact happen in the place where the seed has fallen, and once to tell it that the ledge has not crumbled away since last time and that the probability is that it will not do so before the seedling has had time to grow, flower and itself set seed a few times. This is not dormancy, one might say, merely an extension of the normal germination process.

All this may sound like splitting hairs. 'Whichever way you put it', you might say, 'the darn things still take their time'. Yes indeed, but 'dormancy' is perhaps a convenient pillow on which to rest the head of reason, and it is still necessary to continue searching for the combinations of factors that govern germination and learn how to apply them. Is carbon dioxide a factor? Are there detector mechanisms for levels of soil chemicals? Others more learned will probably have a much better idea of the possible equations. Meanwhile, as there is much thought to be done and experiments to be performed, and it is likely to take many years, we will have to carry on with the practices that have produced results in the past.

3

DEFEATING DORMANCY

Or how to cheat nature

The trouble with patience is that for most of us it is in short supply. So is space. With just a few (or even a couple) of frames, then, how can we overcome this problem of dormancy in seeds and maximize our success rate? If the long-term solution is frustratingly fraught with problems and the results of our own shortcomings, is there a short-term one?

Well, yes, there is. It is possible to break the various dormancy mechanisms, but you need to know how and it helps a good deal if you have some idea of why you should apply this or that method to one kind of seed or another.

I want to emphasize at this stage that raising plants from seed is essentially a simple matter. It is a magical way of introducing children to gardening and something everyone can do. There is no better way of putting your hand in the hand of nature and coming intimately into contact with the life-force of the natural world. On the other hand, as a discerning and improving gardener, you will want to get the best results possible, and the methods we are about to look at are to this end. They are not essential to the enjoyment of seed-sowing but do help a lot. To put things into their true perspective, the majority of seeds of wild species from non-tropical parts of the world, including plants from which our vegetables are derived, have dormant seeds. Highly bred flowers and vegetables, however, tend to have had the dormancy bred out of them, chiefly because it is much easier to carry out ultra-long-term breeding programmes with the least amount of lost time, and also because the last thing you want with an annual flower or a vegetable is to have to wait for a further year or two after sowing. On the other hand, a relatively small investment in time is well worth it if the end product is a long-lived tree or shrub or herbaceous perennial that can be kept going for decades by splitting it up every couple of years.

DORMANCY IN WARM-CLIMATE SEEDS

You do not need to worry too much about dormancy in seeds from warm climates. After-ripening, which is a kind of dormancy, is taken care of by the fact that there is no point in sowing them in autumn, as you do not want to have to try to get them through their first winter as tiny seedlings. So they are stored and, if stored properly, they will after-ripen nicely in time for being sown in spring. On the other hand, there are some seeds from warm climates that do exhibit dormancy and I'm afraid the only way to know which are which is to rely on someone like me to tell you. In the lists in Chapter 14 you will discover, for example, that the so-called mimosa trees (Australian species of *Acacia*) have hard seed coats and germinate quickly only if soaked for 24 hours in water that starts near to boiling point. Some *Eucalyptus* species such as the spinning gum (*E. perriniana*) and the gum-top stringy bark (*E. delegatensis*) need to have their dormancy broken by cold treatment. They are, however, exceptions and, while it is a good idea mentally to separate your seeds into those from warm and cold climates, you need to bear these odd ones in mind.

DORMANCY IN COLD-CLIMATE SEEDS

Cold-climate seeds are much more likely to be dormant for a while, for reasons we have already discussed. They are the ones upon which we rely for most of our seed-raised outdoor ornamentals and the ones for which we need to know what to expect and why, to avoid being disappointed by the results.

Let's take first the seeds that need to 'know' that winter has been and gone and that spring is really here. Their requirements boil down to being informed that they have passed through one or

Ways of breaking dormancy and accelerating germination

◆ Cold stratification — giving alternating periods of chilling and warming
◆ Treating the seed coat — chipping, abrading, soaking or giving a long period of warmth
◆ Providing bottom heat — soil-warming cables and/or propagators

two quite long periods of chilling cold (but *not* actual freezing), with perhaps a mild spell between, and have finally arrived in the gentle, moist, safe warmth of spring.

As we have seen, we can sow in autumn and let things happen naturally. However, we do not obtain much of our seed until spring and we know, too, that there are dangers to seed and seedlings during the long period from late autumn to early spring.

The old professionals used to lay dormant seeds in layers between layers of moist sand in pits in the garden. The layers, or strata, of seeds and sand gave the operation the name 'stratification', which is still used for the cold treatment of dormant seeds, although few people seem to know why.

Today, the term is used for two operations: the overcoming of seed-coat dormancy, and the breaking of the dormancy inherent in the tissues of the seed. Today's professionals have all sorts of tricks up their sleeves, but these are mostly simple and logical. If they are reduced to an easily managed system for home gardeners they make three separate groups.

GROUP 1 COLD 'STRATIFICATION'

The great majority of alpines and many trees and shrubs have seeds that are deeply dormant because of chemical inhibitors within their tissues. These are changed only by alternating periods of chilling and warming. Notable among them are *Mahonia*, *Sorbus*, *Primula*, *Iris*, *Aster*, *Aconitum*, *Anemone*, *Astrantia*, *Dicentra*, *Cupressus* and many more listed in Chapters 12 and 14.

There are many satisfactory methods of giving seeds an artificial sense of the passing of winter, but the domestic fridge provides one of the best. Preparation is important.

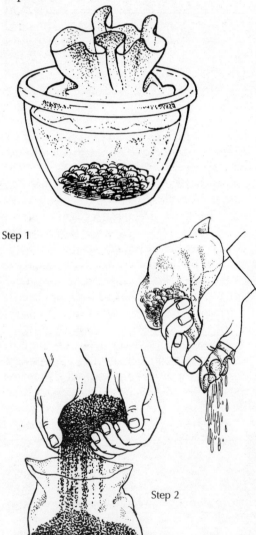

Step 1

Step 2

Step 1
Put the seeds of each subject in a separate polythene bag and add enough cold water to more than cover them. The seeds may float, but don't worry. Let them stand for 24 hours.

Step 2
Gather the bag into a neck with your hand or a piece of string pulled tightly enough round the bag so that you can drain away all the water but not the seeds. Now add just enough of a 50/50 by volume mixture of moist sand and moss peat and mix the seeds with it. It is this mixture you are eventually going to sow, so don't use so much that the seeds will end up deeply buried.

Step 3
Put the bags in the refrigerator. There need be no mess and the bags will not take up much room. The seeds may need to spend as little as

ten days or as long as three months in the fridge, and the only way of telling is to look for signs of germination or consult Chapters 12 and 14. It is a good idea to take them out for 48 hours once or twice during the chilling process.

Step 3

Step 4
When germination begins, or when you feel the need to sow them for a particular reason or because it is getting well on into spring, fill some pots with a soil-less compost and sow the entire contents of each bag on the surface. (This is for everything except alpines, for which a John Innes-type loam-based compost is best.) Label the pots and put them in the frame and wait for the excellent results that you should most reasonably expect. The actual technique of sowing is covered in Chapter 6.

Step 4

GROUP 2 MECHANICAL TREATMENT OF HARD SEED COATS

Many members of the pea family (Leguminosae), which include among their large number the sweet pea (*Lathyrus*), *Acacia*, *Anthyllis*, *Cercis*, *Colutea*, *Cytisus*, *Genista*, *Gleditsia*, *Laburnum*, *Robinia*, *Sophora* and *Wisteria*, have hard seed coats that take a very long time to permit the passage of water into the seed unless they are mechanically broken down. Cannas and members of the mallow family (Malvaceae) have the same characteristic. Germination is speeded up greatly if mechanical methods are used to reduce the resistance of the seed coats.

Very special seeds, such as sweet pea 'Cream Southbourne', arguably the best and most fragrant cream form of all, are worth treating individually. Hold them in a pair of eyebrow tweezers and make a shallow, slicing cut through the seed coat. Locate the hilum (the scar where the seed was attached to the pod) and make the cut

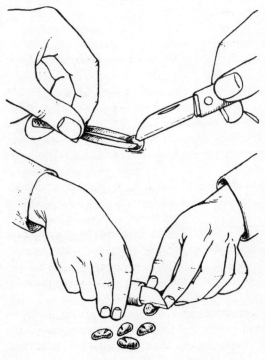

Chipping the seed coat of a small, hard-coated seed. No matter how tempting, you should resist the urge to cut towards yourself. Using tweezers is safe, even if the knife slips. Larger seeds can comfortably be held in the hand, but here you really must cut away from the fingers holding the seed, otherwise you are likely to have an accident. Keep your knife well sharpened: a blunt one is more dangerous than one with a keen edge.

You will probably evolve your own method of abrading hard-coated seeds between sheets of sandpaper, but I prefer to move one sheet in a circular motion upon the other, gradually tipping them to allow the treated seeds to fall into a bowl.

to one side of it – not opposite. This is called chipping. Other, larger seeds can be filed instead.

With smaller seeds a good method is to rub them between sheets of sandpaper. A medium-grade sandpaper will rub away nicely at the seeds and leave you in control. I find that too fine a grade clogs before it does the job, while too coarse a sandpaper grips the seeds too firmly and tends to shoot them in all directions when you finally free them.

We have already seen that seeds of the true acacias germinate best if soaked for 24 hours in water that starts just below boiling point (page 32). The same applies to, among others, *Albizia julibrissin*, *Gleditsia*, *Gymnocladus dioica* (Kentucky coffee tree) and *Rhus*. When you have drained the water off, the seeds are often seen to be surrounded by a jelly, and it is worth washing them again to try to get rid of it, otherwise sowing can become a sticky and inaccurate business.

Professionals go to greater lengths than this, testing the seed first and re-soaking as necessary, but for home gardeners the main aim is to obtain a few plants, rather than commercial quantities.

You need enough to cover yourself for losses later on and for giving away or swapping. More than that can actually be a burden. Many textbooks and other sources that are more theoretical than practical will go into all sorts of practices such as treatment with sulphuric acid, but I must emphasize that these are neither necessary nor desirable at home. Mixing sulphuric acid, for example, is safe in thoroughly experienced hands as long as the right thing – the water or the acid – is added first. Get it the wrong way round and you may be disfigured and blinded for life. I have for the moment forgotten which is which and have no intention whatever of reminding myself.

GROUP 3 TREATMENT OF TOUGH SEED COATS

This group is different from the last because the seed coats will allow water into the seed but prevent germination by refusing to split until a cycle of temperature changes has taken place. Many seeds from berries are like this and include *Cotoneaster*, *Sorbus*, *Crataegus*, *Rosa*, *Sambucus* and *Viburnum* as well as *Acer*, *Elaeagnus*, *Cornus* and many herbaceous plants.

They need to experience quite a long period of warm, summery temperatures, followed by anything up to three months at 0–10°C

Provided that you keep pots of seed well watered, with a sheet of glass firmly keeping a humid atmosphere, you can place them in sun for part of the day to raise the temperature. The glass should be shaded, preferably with white glasshouse shade paint. Clay pots should be shaded, preferably with white glasshouse shade paint.

(32–50°F). This is best achieved by sowing as soon as the seed is ready and placing the pots outside, covered with a sheet of glass. You may well have to wait 18 months or more for results. There are ways of breaking the dormancy involving putting the seed in an airing cupboard and then the fridge, but it has to be said that it all begins to be a bit of a fiddle and you might as well, for this group at any rate, bring your patience into play and go along with nature – the results are usually better in that event, too.

Variations on the methods used to break dormancy and generally accelerate germination are given in the lists in Chapters 13, 14 and 15, but the underlying principles are the same.

BREAKING DORMANCY WITH SOIL HEATING AND PROPAGATORS

The other main aid to assisting germination is not a method of cheating nature as much as kidding her along. The provision of bottom heat brings spring, as it were, a little forward.

I know of few seeds that are not helped by bottom heat as long as the means used is not set at too high a temperature. All sorts of methods have been used, from pouring boiling water into the bottoms of seed drills before sowing to sophisticated under-soil heating and modern heated propagating cases. My own methods have boiled down (if I may use the expression) to looking after the various pre-treatments (chilling, chipping, etc.) first and then bringing everything into frames with under-soil heating cables. It works and I have relatively few failures. I have no hesitation in recommending that you provide it by one means or another as generously as you can, and I would suggest that of your two seed frames one should be heated and that the preferred set-up would be two heated and one unheated, the latter used for weaning.

Tropical seeds that need really high temperatures (such as palms) or high temperatures and very high humidity (busy lizzies for example) are best sown in heated propagators, preferably on a greenhouse bench. With the latter, the method of choice is to wrap the entire pot or tray in clingfilm in order to trap the maximum amount of moisture until germination is more or less complete. Busy lizzie seeds, unless so treated, can be among the most reluctant of all to germinate. It may be a long way from them to alpines but the problem is the same: how to persuade seeds that nature is operating as normal. Successful seed-raising is to a large extent one big confidence trick, but it is an honest one in the context of gardening – which is, after all, the art of acclimatizing nature to an artificial environment.

HARVESTING AND STORING SEED

Or how to avoid spoiling everything before you even start

The great majority of seeds sown in home gardens come from seed companies, often known as seed houses. As gardeners progress, they tend to add another source – seeds from their own gardens and those of friends. The next stage is to join one or more horticultural societies with general or specialist seed lists, and the last is to contact botanical gardens all round the world and join their seed distribution schemes, which have the advantage of usually being free.

Wherever your seeds come from, they must arrive at the sowing bench alive, healthy and raring to go. You may think that sounds easy but in fact it is anything but and the great seed houses spend a great deal of their energy and financial substance on constantly testing and re-testing the procedures that bring good seed to your frames and propagators.

SEEDS FROM PLANT TO PACKET

With an international seed house such as Thompson & Morgan of Ipswich, England, which supplies gardeners in the United States and Australia and many other parts of the world in addition to its home market, the harvesting, storing, packing and despatching process is under constant review. There are a great many variable factors that influence how well plants set seed. For example, climatic differences at harvesting time can have a substantial influence on germination rates. Come what may, seed has to arrive in first-class condition at the customer, no matter where he or she may be.

The seeds you sow may have been harvested a very long way away. For example, seed of *Viola wittrockiana* (garden pansies) is obtained from growers in Germany and France but the F_1 varieties come from Japan. Sweet peas, sunflowers and French marigolds are grown in California, while many peas originate in New Zealand.

Plants from Thompson & Morgan's fields are picked in summer and autumn and laid on palettes in a greenhouse or polytunnel to dry thoroughly. The seed is taken from the plants and cleaned by hand – a process known as winnowing. It is then placed in a cloth bag or sack (depending on the size of the seed) and taken to a dry store. Seed from outside suppliers and contractors arrives at this stage.

The dry store at Thompson & Morgan's Ipswich headquarters contains seed from every corner of the world. It is kept at 20°C (68°F) all year round, which is much warmer than you should keep your seeds. The secret is the low humidity (20 per cent), which keeps the seeds dry enough to enable the maintenance of a temperature high enough for people to work comfortably while keeping the seed in first-class condition.

In the store, each batch of seed is booked in and given a number, which remains with it for life (one to three years or occasionally more), whether it is sold by mail order or in retail packets. As soon as it is booked in, two samples are taken. One is sent to the T&M laboratory for germination testing only, and the other goes to the trial-grounds supervisor for growing under normal conditions.

When the germination test is finished it is given the go-ahead or the thumbs down. If the latter, a re-test is done from the same batch. If it is from an outside supplier and it fails again, the seed is sent back to the supplier and a new lot is purchased. If it is from Thompson & Morgan's own plants it may be re-tested again and if the same result is reached the seed is rejected and not used.

If the seed is passed, it is put into production. Some eight million packets of seed every year are filled by hand by about 75 people from Ipswich and surrounding areas. With Thompson &

Morgan (but not all companies) it is sent for foiling before being put into packets. All Thompson & Morgan seeds are packed in foil as it keeps the seed in better condition than any other material, insulating it from temperature fluctuations and any dampness that might occur during transit. Every foil pack carries the batch number given to the seed when it was booked in and this number is also printed on the outside of the packet when it is sealed so that it can be traced back if there are any complaints about germination. If any such complaint is received, another germination test is automatically carried out. All Thompson & Morgan stock seed (that which is on the shelves of the cool, dry warehouse ready for despatch by mail order or to retail outlets) is tested for germination twice each year.

In the days when germination tests were less precise than they are now, and when your local grocer had a rack of seed packets of doubtful age and chequered history, gardeners did well to treat many of them with suspicion. The great names in the seed industry came through while others disappeared, largely due to a constant watch being kept on quality. Nowadays we can have confidence in what we are buying.

HARVESTING SEED

It is great fun to harvest your own seed and see it through to a satisfactory germination. In the next chapter you will see that, although with a great many plants it is a waste of time to do this, with those for which it is appropriate – mainly *species* of ornamental plants other than annuals – it is highly satisfying.

Harvest time starts in summer and goes on well into autumn. Seeds vary in size from that of quail's eggs to ground pepper; some such as hydrangeas wait to be shaken from the flower heads; some simply fall; others such as magnolias dangle awhile from threads of mucus, while yet others, including hardy geraniums and violas, ping away into the undergrowth without a moment's warning. Catching samples of all of them takes ingenuity, observation, and a trip round the garden once a day after mid-summer, which is no bad thing from several points of view.

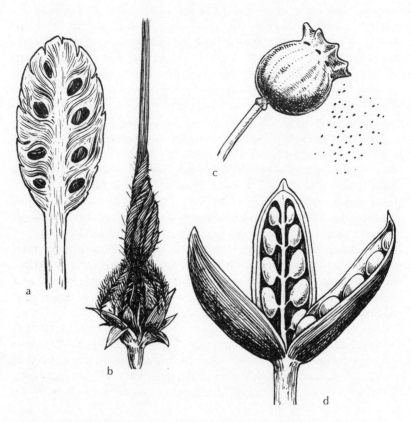

Seeds at the critical point where they should be harvested before they are lost.

(a) Magnolia seeds – once you see one or two seeds, which are usually red or orange, dangling from ribbons of silk, you can open the sausage-like pod and remove the rest;

(b) Erodium seeds (alpines closely related to hardy geraniums) 'unfurl' as they dry and are carried on the wind;

(c) Poppies – as the seed pod becomes increasingly dry, seeds are shaken out as if from a pepper pot;

d) Iris seeds are slower to disperse but are ripe just after the pod begins to split.

SEED GATHERING

Seeds are best gathered in paper bags. (Most envelopes are no good because they leak at the corners, but self-sealing wages envelopes – the kind without windows – are excellent for storage of seed later on.) A good supply of paper bags from bar-of-chocolate size to a few large enough to put a hat in is the first thing with which to stock up.

The stems of some plants should be cut before the seed is quite ready and can be laid on a bench or in a shallow box or tray in an airy, warm place to dry. Irises, incarvilleas, poppies (including *Meconopsis*) and many more whose seeds disappear rapidly once the capsule opens can be treated in this way. Hardy geraniums, irises, euphorbias (especially the honey-scented, tender *Euphorbia mellifera*) and others that on a hot day suddenly explode their seed capsules and fling the seed some distance away, should have their flower heads or stems collected when almost ready and put upside down in large paper bags. The necks of the bags should be tied and you can then have fun listening to the explosions and, in the case of the euphorbias, actually seeing the bag jump.

The complete seed heads of plants with very tiny seeds, such as hydrangeas, which are at the pepper-size end of the range (collect only species, not garden varieties) should be put in paper bags in the same way. Every other day or so, give the seed head a shake, and you will end up with a little heap of seed complete with the odd tiny weevil or minute beetle.

Larger seeds can be dried and then put straight into storage envelopes, but many of them are the better for being sown straight away. Among these are oaks, magnolias and any seeds with a high moisture content. You can usually tell these by their generally softer feel. They may be leathery rather than pebble-hard, slightly greasy to the touch, and usually large. Many tree seeds are best sown as soon as ready: how to do it is covered in Chapter 5.

WINNOWING

Most seeds will have to be separated from their seed coats or containers and any bits of leaf or stem which may have been collected with them. This process is winnowing. Have ready some sheets of clean white paper, at least A4 size. Don't bother with sieves.

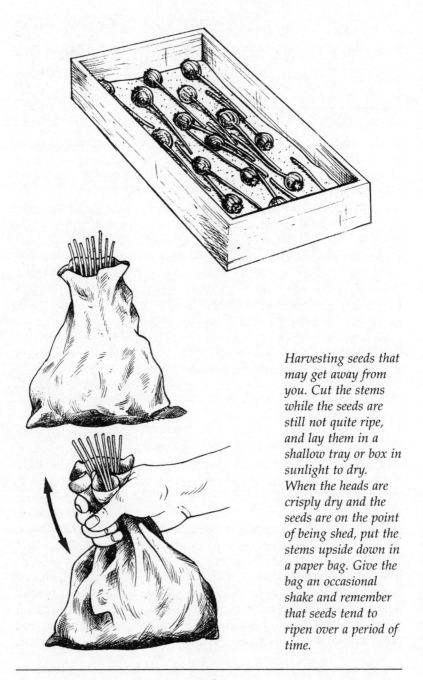

Harvesting seeds that may get away from you. Cut the stems while the seeds are still not quite ripe, and lay them in a shallow tray or box in sunlight to dry. When the heads are crisply dry and the seeds are on the point of being shed, put the stems upside down in a paper bag. Give the bag an occasional shake and remember that seeds tend to ripen over a period of time.

Winnowing methods

◆ Roll seed heads between the hands to loosen the debris
◆ Pour small seeds onto paper and tilt and shake to separate
seeds and chaff
◆ Blow gently onto small seeds with lightweight debris

I cannot think how many times I have read instructions to obtain a range of sieves of different mesh sizes but it is absolute nonsense. Sieves clog, get bashed in so that they develop flat bits and corners, and are never the right size. This is not surprising, as nature does not order seeds into neat categories of size, and to do the job half-way properly you would need a great many sieves. Fingers, hands, dexterity and gentle breath are all you need for winnowing seed.

Smaller seeds will have to be winnowed away from the material of the capsule or whatever sort of vessel they developed in. There is such a huge variety of such arrangements that I can only give you a general idea of technique, but it should be enough to make you feel happy to tackle anything. First, though, never allow your hands to come into prolonged contact with any sap whatever, and, whenever dealing with seeds that need to be extracted from pods that are still crisp and sappy, always wear glasses or goggles. You never know how sensitive you may be to various plants – something for which I can vouch, having lost the entire skin off the palm of one hand from harvesting seed of *Helleborus orientalis*.

If you can, always winnow material that is dry and wash your hands with soap and hot water afterwards. Leave really poisonous plants such as *Aconitum* well alone and treat only non-toxic seeds. Where seed heads contain a lot of dry stuff among which the seeds are embedded, roll them between the palms of your hands over one of your sheets of white paper, which you have previously folded in half and opened up again. The seeds should rain down while most of the debris remains in your hands. Some flakes and shards will fall through, however, and these will lie with the seeds in the trough made when you folded the paper. Pick up the paper and tilt it this way and that along the crease until the seeds make a pile in the middle. Shake the paper so that the pile spreads along the trough and then again into the centre. After a short while you will find that the seeds are in the middle and the unwanted bits at

Different methods of winnowing seeds.

(a) The dried seed heads are rolled between the palms of the hands so that the seed becomes detached and falls between the fingers onto a sheet of paper.

(b) Tilting and gently shaking material so that the seeds remain on the paper and the debris falls below.

(c) When larger seeds are accompanied by light debris, this may be gently blown away.

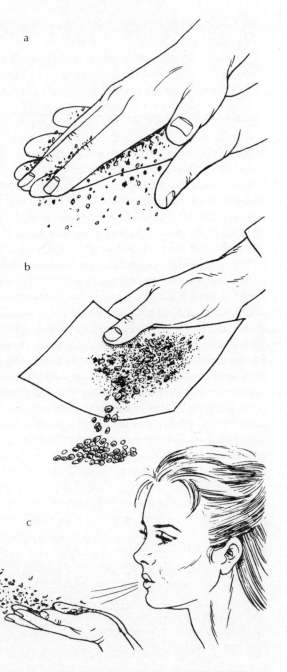

the ends, and you can get rid of these with the tip of your finger or an artist's paintbrush.

This system of winnowing works well for almost everything. The pepper-like hydrangea seeds, or the slightly larger ones of meconopsis, can be poured directly onto the paper and the tilting and shaking process carried out.

Andrew Tokely, the Trial Grounds Supervisor at Thompson & Morgan, has a method of cleaning seed that is highly efficient but very simple. Take two A4 manila envelopes and put one on top of the other. This gives a stiff but bendable board. Bend it along one side so that the whole forms a J shape. Put the seed in the trough formed by the lower part of the J and throw it upwards a couple of inches, catching it back in the J again. With a background of clean paper on a table in front of you, you can see the debris flying over the far edge of the J, leaving the clean seed behind. Andrew says you shouldn't be afraid to bounce the seed: any that is lost was probably ultra-light and no good anyway. Work under as bright a light as possible.

You should winnow everything. It is no joke in spring to find families of busy weevils grinning happily up at you, nurtured on the embryos from your precious seeds, or to have several earwigs dash out, making you jump out of your skin and cast the seed to the four corners of the potting shed. One little bit of dead plant material, already infected with a fungus (as it almost certainly will be) can ruin an entire batch of seed. That little bit of extra care is worth ... well, who knows? It may be a grove of paulownias, a drift of exotic Australian bottle-brushes or potentially the only three plants in cultivation of *Exoticum ultimum.*

SEED STORAGE

Having made sure your seeds are dry and clean, seal them in their paper wage envelopes and put them in a wooden box with the lid lightly closed – *not* a tin box with the lid on, and *never* in plastic bags. You may like to take a leaf out of Thompson & Morgan's book and save up all your chocolate-bar foils over the year and use them to wrap your seeds in within their envelopes. Whatever

Storage methods

◆ Put winnowed seed into paper, wages-type envelopes and label
◆ Seed could be wrapped first in chocolate bar foil
◆ Store envelopes in a wooden box in a cool, dry place, preferably with some silica gel crystals

method you use, store the packets in a really cool place where it is dry – truly dry. Dampness is death to seeds; warm dampness is very rapid death. It is a good idea to put a few silica gel crystals in the box. They will absorb any dampness and when they become fully charged with moisture you can dry them out in the oven (set at 120°C/250°F/Gas mark 1/2) for about 20 minutes.

LABELLING

I suppose here is as good a place as any to deliver the first of my lectures on labelling (part two is on page 63). Unlabelled seed is entirely useless. You simply *must* label everything. Once more, take your cue from Thompson & Morgan and label each batch from the moment it is harvested. Even if you know perfectly well that it is *Incarvillea delavayi*, label it as soon as you have gathered the stems. If you don't, and you grow *I. mairei* as well, you will inevitably mix them up, which would be a pity as the former is twice as tall as the latter, flowers later and is red rather than pink.

Label with the name and the date when the seed was harvested. If there are any other notes, such as 'white' or 'the one from Mrs Overthefence', make sure you have a system for carrying these through the lives of the seeds as well. After all, you can write a veritable biography on the face of a paper packet. And when you sow any seed of whatever kind – ornamental or vegetable – always add a label to every pot, not just the first of two or three. This will save you grief when the pots eventually get mixed up as surely and inevitably as kids always get lost on the last day of a holiday.

5

WHAT TO SOW – AND WHAT NOT TO SOW

Or how to make the best use of your time

PLANTS FROM SEEDS OR CUTTINGS?

Species – that is to say plants derived unchanged from the wild populations – come true from seed (which means that the seedlings are very closely similar to one another) as long as they have not hybridized – something which occurs when two or more species cross-breed. Sometimes, however, one individual will be different and more garden-worthy than the usual seedlings. It may be of a different colour, for instance. It may then be given a fancy name to come after its Latin one. If you sow seed of this different plant, almost all the resulting seedlings will be the same as the wild form or show minute differences, but none (or at best one in several hundreds or even thousands) will be closely similar to the different plant. If you take cuttings or divisions of the different plant, all the offspring will be exactly alike – in fact, clones.

On the other hand, if you sow seed of sweet pea 'Maggie May', you can expect every flower on every plant to have a rich fragrance and elegantly wavy petals of light sky blue flushed with white. Any other result should have you down on Thompson & Morgan like a ton of bricks, as it is exclusive to them and that is how they describe it. 'Maggie May' and the selected seedling such as I have described above are both cultivars (botanese for 'cultivated variety'), but the results from seed are entirely different in each case.

The point of all this is that you will suffer acute disappointment if one day your *Camellia japonica* 'Alba Plena' sets seed and you sow it, happily hoping for lots of little 'Alba Plenas'. Instead, the seedlings that result will probably have very small, red flowers with nine petals each instead of large, white ones with about 100 each. On the other hand, every plant of *Nicotiana* 'Lime Green' will look the same when grown from seed because of generation after generation of breeding for the colour, making the chances of a 'rogue' seedling very small.

Let's look at another example, that of *Viola* 'Irish Molly'. This is a green-faced viola with brownish-goldish markings that is quietly gorgeous. Someone raised lots of seedlings and distributed them as 'Irish Molly', but each was subtly different to the next and to Molly herself. This happened again and again until it was feared the original plant had disappeared beneath the weight of impostors. Luckily it was found again and is now propagated by cuttings, so it is now a clonal cultivar, not a seed-bred one. But if you'd had some of the seedlings, would you have known?

The fault is in the term 'cultivar', which is the official word covering what you and I tend to call garden varieties. Perhaps serious consideration should be given by the botanical authorities to providing us with two new terms so that clonal cultivars and seed-bred ones could be readily differentiated. Meanwhile, we have to work out our own way of knowing which garden varieties can be sown to come 'true' and which have to be propagated by cuttings, division, layers and other vegetative means.

WHICH METHOD OF PROPAGATION?

The best general guide is that garden varieties of perennial plants – in the true sense, meaning plants that can flower for two or more years, and covering trees, shrubs, bulbs, herbaceous perennials, top fruit, soft fruit and most alpines – are clonal cultivars and must be propagated by vegetative means (such as by taking cuttings). This is necessary because their seeds will produce plants completely unlike their parents. Seed-bred cultivars, on the other hand, are just about all annuals, biennials and vegetables. Seed from these will be like the parent.

It is thus worth sowing seed of species of perennial plants, but not of their garden varieties or hybrids. You will know species by their names, which consist of two Latin words only and have no 'fancy' names in a vernacular language. Always label your plants and keep the labels legible, otherwise when it comes to harvesting your own seeds you will not know which are worth taking.

It is also worth sowing all seed offered in seed catalogues (you may be glad to hear!) but, except in certain cases, it is *not* worth sowing the seed which these plants may then set in your garden.

These exceptions are what are termed 'inbreeders', usually vegetables that have a natural tendency to breed within the same line. These include lettuce, peas, french beans and swedes. However, I would suggest you don't save seed even of these, because of the great general increase in the use of F_1 hybrids.

F_1 HYBRIDS

These are created by plant breeders, who first develop strongly inbreeding lines and then take two of them and hybridize them. The result is called the first filial generation, or F_1 , and the offspring are of uniform colour and quality and usually have higher yields (vegetables) or bear significantly more flowers. If you save seed of the F_1 generation, the offspring are termed F_2, or second

Which method of propagation is best for which type of plant?

◆ Garden varieties of perennial plants – trees, shrubs, bulbs, herbaceous plants, soft fruit and many alpines – will have been propagated vegetatively. Seed from them will not come true, that is, seedlings will not be like the parents.
◆Perennial species – plants that have been derived unchanged from wild populations – are what you will find in catalogues. Sow these, but any seed from the plants will not breed true. Sow seed from annuals and many vegetables and it *will* breed true.

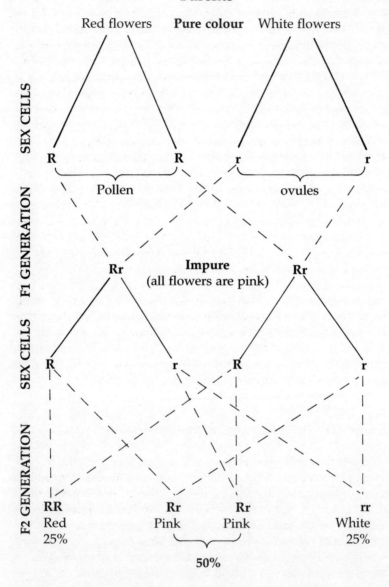

Parents

Red flowers **Pure colour** **White flowers**

SEX CELLS

R   R   r   r

Pollen   ovules

F1 GENERATION

Rr   **Impure**   Rr
(all flowers are pink)

SEX CELLS

R   r   R   r

F2 GENERATION

RR   **Rr**   **Rr**   **rr**
Red   Pink   Pink   White
25%   25%

50%

Genetic diagram showing how pairs of characters are transmitted to the F₁ and F₂ generations.

filial generation. These will not be uniform and may vary considerably. They may be very good plants, but the results are unpredictable. Seed houses in fact offer many items that are non-F_1, such as *Nicotiana* 'Lime Green', but they know their full histories and are confident that the results of sowing them will be, if not uniform, then very close to it or acceptably similar to one another.

You might conclude that it is in the interests of a seed house to offer as many F_1 hybrids as possible, as you will have to go back to them for next year's seed. But, of course, the company *is* providing you with the best possible product and has spent a great deal of research effort on producing it. At least they do not do what Joseph Latour Marliac (1830–1911) did. He was the first raiser of hybrid water-lilies and supplied the painter Monet with what were then quite astonishing plants. Nobody knew how he did it and it was only very recently that papers came to light showing that, after they had set seed, he destroyed his F_1 generation hybrids between hardy and tropical water-lilies. He then chose the best of the F_2 generation, named them, and propagated them by division. People who tried to copy his work by sowing seed of these clonal cultivars failed dismally because they had no clue as to the parentage of the parents of the plants they raised, none of which were anything like the plants sold by the Latour Marliac nursery.

HOW MUCH SEED TO SOW?

Whatever seed you sow, from whatever source, try to avoid sowing too much of an item. In many cases you will be lucky to obtain an amount that will give you more than just a few plants but, in general, just a few is all you will need anyway. On the other hand, batches of many kinds of small seeds, though comparable only with a pinch of salt, are capable of producing hundreds of seedlings. I once raised enough seedlings of *Paulownia tomentosa* to furnish one hectare ($2^1/_2$ acres) of land with closely planted foxglove trees. Needless to say, I did not pot many of them up, and in subsequent years sowed a small fraction of the amount.

It is immensely tempting to go on gathering seed far beyond any amount that is sensible. Try not to do this and take just enough for yourself, friends, and perhaps the seed exchange of any garden club or society to which you belong. If you take too much you are just about certain to sow too much, taking up room that could be occupied by other items. You will also be tempted to sow too thickly which, as we shall see, is poor practice indeed.

If there is nothing to do but to throw the surplus seed away, do so, but you might find it worthwhile storing the remainder for another year just in case on the one hand you have a disaster and lose all your seedlings (woodlice, slugs and so on) and on the other you find the seed-set was a one-off, which is something that can happen. I once found a heavy set of seed on the pineapple broom (*Cytisus battandieri*), a most uncommon event, sowed enough for a commercial quantity of seedlings, and gave the rest away. During the following decade it never happened again.

VEGETABLES FROM SEED

When it comes to vegetables, you must take a position concerning their importance in your life. You need to ask yourself first if you really do want to grow them, then which ones, then why, and lastly whether you have room.

If you love the ultra-fresh, crisp juiciness of vegetables straight from the garden, if you believe that the more organic approach taken by most home gardeners produces enhanced flavour, if you feel that growing vegetables materially assists the family budget, if the regimented ranks of vegetables appeals strongly to you, and if you simply enjoy the whole business of growing veg, then most of your questions are already answered and how you go about things will depend on the space available.

WHICH VEGETABLES TO GROW?

Nowadays, however, developments in the marketing of vegetables have had a considerable influence on gardeners. Some (and I am among them) feel that what space we have should be devoted to those vegetable varieties with especially fine flavour and quality seldom seen in the shops – French salad potatoes such as 'Pink Fir Apple', 'Charlotte' and 'Kipfler', F_1 tomato 'Sweet 100', F_1 sweet pepper 'Gypsy' and the sensationally superior dwarf bean 'Masai', for example. You might even think that a separate veg garden is not for you and that you would like to grow the vegetables mixed among the ornamental plants. Beets, chards, runner beans, lettuces such as 'Lollo Rossa' and many other vegetables are highly decorative and blend in well in the general garden, particularly if the style is somewhat cottagey.

On the whole, most gardeners who find themselves dismissing vegetable gardening as not really their thing would do well to pause and read through today's vegetable catalogues. It is difficult to do so without at least deciding that, well yes, just these few varieties are so tempting that room for them really must be found.

The reason for growing some of your own is that, while advances in importing vegetables in good condition from places like Israel and Kenya have indeed transformed the shelves of the stores, great strides have also been made in the development of vegetable cultivars for the home garden. There is nothing in the world to compare with a fresh Supersteak tomato sliced in vinaigrette with chopped basil; no way a radish from the supermarket has the tangy essence of summer of one that comes straight from the ground, and nothing to compare with 'Hopkins Fenlander' celery, next to which so many imported kinds are mere watery string.

SOMETHING NOT TO GROW?

Take care not to become embroiled in fashion and faddery. A garden is an artificial environment. It is not a place in which to encourage weeds. 'Wildflower' seeds may sound like something with which you can make a contribution to the environment, but they are very difficult to grow and are often simply undesirable. If you have a very large garden with a grassy drift in which wild flowers could be encouraged to grow prettily and unaggressively, by all means go ahead. But don't go sowing nettles, harebells, speedwells and others that can spoil life not only for you but for your neighbours as well. Do bear in mind that many cultivated plants are natives of the country you live in – snakeshead fritillaries and Tenby daffodils in Britain, trilliums, penstemons and phloxes in America – and that all plants are natives or decendants of natives of somewhere on the planet. Growing plants is a way to help the environment: growing well-chosen plants from seed is a way to feel part of it.

It has to be said, though, that you are of course fully entitled to grow whatever you please, as long as it is neither on the one hand illegal nor on the other a nuisance. Nobody can tell you what you ought or ought not to grow and nobody should attempt to impose their ideas of gardening upon you. On the other hand, there are wise courses and unwise ones, profitable ways of going about things and ways that bring sad disappointment; there is good gardening and bad. Good choices will bring you fulfilment and a fine garden; ill-advised ones will spoil your enjoyment and frustrate your hopes.

6

SOWING AND GROWING (1): POTS AND CONTAINERS

Or how to succeed from seed tray to garden

The great majority of seeds can all be sown in the same way. I use a standard method for them and I recommend it to you because it works. I only vary it for seeds that must have special treatment or are sown in the open ground.

The standard method applies to all seeds except for (a) alpines, (b) primulas, (c) house and greenhouse plants, which need higher temperatures and are best sown in pots put in propagators with the temperatures set to the level recommended in your seed catalogue or, if none is mentioned, between 24 and 26°C (75–80°F), and (d) all seeds that are sown in the open ground, which includes many vegetables and most hardy annuals. In the lists within Chapters 14 and 15 you will find details of special treatments for seeds that need more than the standard method.

SOWING IN WARMTH

I use bottom heat set at about 20°C (68°F) or a little less, except (as mentioned above) for house and greenhouse plants and alpines and primulas, which are better off without it. Other cold-country seeds, sown earlier, are first given a spell without heat.

Bottom heat is not expensive to install and run. It is so worthwhile in terms of the wide range of plants you can raise with it that you should consider it very seriously. Remember, though, that it is an aid to germination only and that you must provide frames or room on a greenhouse bench for weaning from the close, warm, humid atmosphere of the germination frame to a much airier, cooler one.

THE GROWING MEDIUM

I use soil-less composts to a large extent but not for seeds that are likely to take a year or two to germinate or which have to stay in the seed tray or pot for a long time before being moved on. Thus I prefer a John Innes type of soil-based seed compost for alpines (for which I add a generous extra amount of sharp grit) and for many bulbs, including dwarf cyclamen, which need to stay put for a couple of years. Some tropicals, such as *Spathiphyllum*, are better in a soil-based compost, but they are in a small minority.

Pots are better than seed trays when using soil-less compost, as the greater its area the more it has a tendency to sink and create puddles into which seed is easily washed, ruining your nice, even, thin sowings.

The soil-less composts give anything up to 20 per cent better germination, all things being equal, than soil-based ones, except in the sorts of cases I have mentioned. I must emphasize 'all things being equal', as there are so many factors bearing on germination that you must be sure none of them is having an effect before assessing the results. Although you should not take my findings as having scientific or even statistical authority, they are nevertheless the result of almost four decades of constant seed-sowing.

Which growing medium?

◆ Soil-less compost. This is good for seed which will germinate the same season. It generally gives good germination rates.
◆ Soil-based compost. Good for seed which takes a long time to germinate. Preferable (with added grit) for alpines.

SOWING TECHNIQUES

Step 1   Filling the pots

Take a small, clean seed tray or pot suitable for the amount of seed of the item you want to sow. It is often a very good idea to use standard-sized (7.5cm/3in), square-section plastic pots, as they will make the most of the room in your frames and only seldom will a home gardener find the need for anything larger.

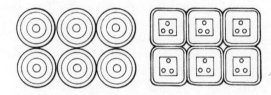

Square pots provide more soil area for the same number.

Fill each one with soil-less compost. You should choose one with a texture that is firm and not slimy to the touch but also not too fibrous. A compost that is not fibrous enough will lie wet and airless, while too much coarse fibre is impossible to work with accurately. The compost should contain sand or some other drainage medium. Just because it says 'compost' on the bag does not necessarily mean that it is suitable for seeds. Read the label carefully. 'Potting' composts and 'all-purpose' composts contain too much fertilizer for tender young seedlings. Make sure that the one you choose specifies that it is for seed-sowing.

I am a great believer of the power of the sensitive hand in successful horticulture and use my fingers to press the compost down in the pot and level it off. It is almost impossible to tell you how much to firm the compost: it is a matter of feel. However, a fair guide is given if you slowly turn the pot over. If the compost does not slip

When filling a pot by hand, use the fingers to firm the compost. The sense of touch is important in avoiding too much compaction or leaving the compost too loose.

out until the pot is nearly upside down, it is about right. If it remains in, even when you tap it ever so lightly, the compost is too compressed. If it falls out earlier, it is too loose.

Some authorities advocate the use of pieces of wood cut to the shapes and sizes of various pots and trays, each with a handle, with which you are supposed to press the compost down. In practice, unless you use your hands anyway, you will get air pockets in the compost, over which there will either be no seedlings at all or any beginning to grow will swiftly die. What with a collection of sieves that would put Escoffier to shame and enough wooden presses to paddle a war canoe, some potting sheds must look like the hoards of mad collectors rather than havens for practical gardeners.

Whichever way you do it, you absolutely must take care to finish with an even surface and one that is level, otherwise seed will end up being washed into hollows or towards one end or side of the pot, and all your efforts at sowing thinly will go for nothing.

Step 2   Watering

When a batch of pots is filled, put them on the ground. Water them with a fine rose, passing the spray to and fro so that the compost becomes thoroughly moistened but not disturbed. Allow them to drain until you can pick them up without their dripping. They are now ready for the seeds, but there is something to do first.

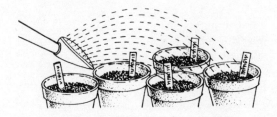

Use the finest rose you can obtain for your watering can.

Step 3   Labelling

This is where part two of the labelling lecture comes in. Label each pot first – before you sow the seed in it – and use a label and marker that will last for years, not weeks or months. Ordinary pencil on anodized aluminium is very good indeed and I have known it last more than 20 years. So-called indelible or 'permanent' pens are anything but, and soon fade to nothing under the influence of ultra-violet light. There is nothing quite so depressing as finding a lush germination in a pot that has been lurking for three years, only to realize that you haven't a clue what it is. Remember, too, that a label has a back and a front, which gives you plenty of room to write the sowing date. This is most important for reasons which, if you have followed my pages so far, will now be obvious. Note, too, that you should write from the blunt end towards the pointed one and not the other way round. The pointed end goes in the compost and you will have to take it out to read it. What is more, rubbing the soil off the writing will tend to make it illegible. It is astonishing how many professional gardeners make this elementary mistake, thorough though their training may have been.

Label everything clearly and accurately. Include the date of sowing and write towards the sharp end of the label. Use ordinary pencil: so-called indelible markers usually last less than one season.

Step 4   Sowing

All manner of gadgetry has been devised for sowing seeds and I have yet to see any that are better than the human hand. I have to say, though, that if you suffer from arthritis or anything else that disables your hands, you may find it a very good idea to investigate various aids. Many people with reduced dexterity use a method involving tapping either the opened packet or a folded piece of paper on which the seed is lying. Gentle tapping as you move the mouth of the packet over the compost enables you to sow remarkably evenly, especially when you become experienced. One gadget, which ejects a seed as you press its top with your thumb, demands more manual skill than a hypodermic, yet is advertized for those with arthritis. Its ultimate fate seems destined to involve being jumped on with a heavy boot.

Sowing directly from the packet is a method that is preferred by many people.

My own way of sowing is to pour the seed into my left hand and pick up a pinch with my right. With a movement rather like the universal sign for money (but upside-down) I then release it from my thumb and first two fingers. I believe this to be a very natural way of ensuring an even sowing and one as thin as I want it to be.

However, others like to hold the seed in one hand and sow pinches of it with the other.

Thin sowing is vital, but this is inhibited when you have over-generous amounts of seed because you feel you should give it the best possible chance and so proceed to sow about ten times as much as you need to. Thick sowing leads to thickly crowded seedlings that grow long and spindly and cannot be pricked out without damage, if they even reach that stage. Damping-off and other fungal diseases are likely to see them off first. Each seed should always have space to develop, the only exception being cluster sowing of annuals such as lobelia, when you prick out each tuft of seedlings and pot them on together.

Step 5   Covering, or not covering

One of the chief stumbling blocks is knowing whether to cover the seed and if so by how much. The general rule is to cover with slightly moist compost to no greater depth than the width of the seed. Although it cannot be applied to large or very small seeds, it is a good rule and one you should try hard to apply. The depth referred to is the one you arrive at after you have lightly pressed down on the compost surface with the flat of your hand.

Larger seeds – anything over about 7mm (^{3}/10in) – should be pressed into the surface of the compost. If the seeds are flat, press them in edgeways until they almost disappear. You will then find that you need very little compost with which to cover them.

It is most important to be in full control when you lightly sprinkle compost over the seeds. It is best to use dry compost for this. Very small seeds should not be covered at all.

With small seeds – a little more than salt-grain size as opposed to ground pepper – you will find it easier to cover with sharp sand. You must, however, hold your hand close to the compost, otherwise the impact of the sand grains bounces the seeds and many will remain uncovered. If you find it difficult, mix the sand and seed together and sow the lot. Many people prefer using sand to covering with compost, as it enables you to see where you have been and helps greatly in achieving an even, thin sowing. It must, however, be clean, washed sand with no clay in it, otherwise it will cap (i.e. become crusted) and become impervious to air.

The sowing sequence

Fill – firm – water – label – sow – cover (sometimes) – rewater.

Step 7   Rewatering

Whichever method you use, once more place the pots on the ground and pass the fine rose over them, this time with particularly great care. The water must not make the slightest puddles on the surface and there should be no washing about of the surface compost or sand. When you have let them drain, put the pots in the frame.

I prefer to stand the pots on the ground outside for watering. If you are not thorough enough, the compost will only be partially moistened, but if you do the job properly indoors there will be a lot of water on the floor.

Step 8   Pricking out

The emerging young seedlings then have to be transplated into individual pots. The usual advice is to prick seedlings out when they show their first pair of true leaves. It is a good general principle but you must use common sense when the true leaves are tiny or do not come in pairs (in conifers they tend to be in whorls). Better, I think, is to suggest that you transplant when the seedlings are just large enough to handle but, in the case of large seedlings, have at least one pair of true leaves.

I still deeply mourn my beloved ivory crochet hook, which I lost 20 years ago. With it I
must have pricked out many thousands of
seedlings. It was better than any of the twee giz-
mos sold nowadays for the job, though probably
no better than a plastic hook. I have met quite a
few wild elephants and don't like the ivory
trade, so would be perfectly happy to use a
series of short-lived plastic crochet hooks but
have never had the heart to. I find myself
instead grabbing the nearest thing, from a spatula to a diary pencil. Whatever you use, make
sure it is slender but strong and does not have a
sharp point.

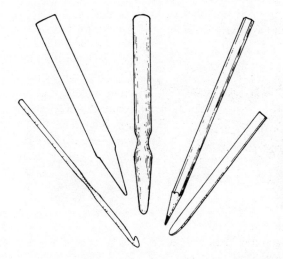

*Suitable tools for
pricking out: (from
left to right) crochet
hook, rigid plant
label, thin stick,
pencil and narrow
spatula.*

Hold the seedling by one of the seed leaves
(cotyledons) or, with those that have only one
seed leaf, by just one of the true leaves. Never
hold the stem. The slightest pressure can cause
enough internal damage severely to weaken the
seedling if not to kill it. Always assume that the
roots are extremely sensitive to damage and lift
them intact and with as little disturbance as possible. As soon as you can, take the weight of the

seedling with the hand in which you are holding the dibber. I usually end up with the seed
leaf between the thumb and forefinger of my
left hand, while the roots rest on the last two
fingers – much the same position as when you
offer your ticket to the slot in the car-park
machine. How you do it does not matter, but
damage at this stage is easy to inflict and ruins
all the trouble you have taken up to this point.

(a) Tackle one seedling at a time unless, as with edging lobelias, it is
best to transplant clumps of seedlings.

(b) Hold a seedling by a leaf or seed leaf, never by the stem.

(c) Take the weight of the seedling and its root system by using the
fingers. This ensures there is no strain on the stem.

The pricking out procedure

Fill pots with suitable compost. Tease out a seedling; hold it by a seed leaf and support it on your hand; lower it into a finger-made hole in the pot; firm it in; label; water gently.

I always make a hole in the compost in the receiving pot or tray with my finger. It is more sensitive than a wooden dibber or pencil and I seem better able to judge its depth to match the dimensions of the seedling in my other hand. Carefully put the seedling upright into the hole and gently firm the soil round it. Don't plant it too shallowly. Often it can be quite a bit deeper than it was in the seed pot, even to the extent of having its seed leaves resting on the surface of the compost. Label each pot.

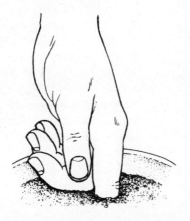

Because the sense of touch is important in avoiding too much compaction or leaving the compost too loose, many good seed-raisers prefer to use their finger rather than a dibber when transplanting seedlings.

When pricking out, use a soil-less compost again unless you are dealing with seedlings grown in a soil-based one, and do not water until you have completed the transplant operation. Moist compost is messy and inaccurate to work with. After the first few times you will soon find yourself adjusting for the sinking that results from firming and watering and will be producing batches of beautifully, evenly potted young plants.

Step 9   Into the frame

Put the pots into a frame, which you should keep closed for a few days to let the seedlings adjust, before opening it slightly by day and gradually increasing the exposure until the frame is permanently open. When fine roots begin to show through the bottoms of the pots, planting time has arrived and you pass from concern with seeds and seedlings into the more general world of plant care.

Once the seedling is transplanted, the compost should be firmed with the fingers. Firm but gentle is the keynote to success with seedlings.

7

SOWING AND GROWING (2): OPEN GROUND

Or taking a risk in an unprotected world

Hardy annuals and most vegetables are sown out of doors where they are to grow. Professionals also grow many trees and shrubs in outdoor seed beds, largely because of restrictions of space. Doing so also deals effectively with dormancy and with seeds that need to be sown as soon as they are ripe because of their low viability. However, most home gardeners who sow tree and shrub seed do so in frames because they do not need large numbers of plants and prefer the greater control they have over just a few seeds and seedlings.

HARDY ANNUALS

Hardy annuals are plants that complete their life-cycles in one year but are hardy in the climate in which they are to grow. Calendulas, cornflowers, stocks and nasturtiums are examples, and you could make an entire bedding scheme using only hardy annuals.

GROUND PREPARATION

It is essential to prepare the ground properly if you are going to enjoy anything less than a nightmare with hardy annuals – and even then you can find yourself plagued with weed seedlings. If your garden is recently converted from meadow, as it probably is if it is a new one, it is a good idea to forget about hardy annuals until three or more years of good gardening with other kinds of plants have gone by. Then it is much less likely that you will find your seedlings swamped by things like redleg, fat hen, docks, thistles and a horde of other 'wildflowers'.

First the bed must be dug to rid it of every trace of root of any perennial weeds, especially those with running roots or underground stems. Then the soil will have to be broken down and raked until you achieve a fine tilth – this is a surface layer of crumbly but slightly floury, smooth, flat soil. New gardens made in clay soils are usually much more difficult to deal with, neither breaking down into a suitable tilth nor being free of dense masses

Digging is not everyone's favourite occupation, so take your time, be patient, and make sure every last piece of perennial weed root has been discovered and removed. Try to dig so that your back is in lordosis – its natural position with a slight concavity in the small of the back. If you round your back outwards all the time as shown above, you will develop injury and pain.

Raking over the soil on a dry, warm day will gradually produce a crumbly texture, often called a tilth.

of the worst perennial weeds imaginable. However, a couple of seasons of careful digging, incorporating as much organic material as you can lay hands on, should see matters right.

PLANNING THE SOWING AREA

So, you will one day find yourself with an area of soil suitable for the job. It is a good idea, once you have established the tilth, to mark out areas for each kind of plant by outlining them with a trickle of sand. Within each area you then draw shallow drills with a pointed stick and sow your seeds evenly in them. You then lightly rake or press the soil into the drills to cover the seeds and give a light watering.

The drills do not have to be in straight lines and can be curved, but the main thing is to draw them in recognizably geometrical patterns. This is because the seeds will germinate along with weed seeds and you will know that the seedlings in the lines are what you want to keep and that everything else must go.

(a) *Drills within the area can easily be marked out with a stick: use a long one and you will not trouble your back.*

(b) *Hardy annuals: mark out the area to be sown with one variety, using a trickle of sand.*

(c) *Sow the seeds in the drills.*

(d) *The seedlings that all look alike and are confined to the drills are the plants; others are weeds and can be pulled up with safety.*

Pre-preparation for annuals

◆ Dig over to remove all roots of perennial weeds
◆ Break down large soil lumps
◆ Dig in as much organic matter as possible
◆ Rake to produce a fine tilth

You can then thin out the seedlings to the desired intervals – nobody I know ever manages to sow them thus – but if you broadcast them you will set yourself all sorts of problems. Not that problems will pass you by if you do the job entirely right. Cats are drawn to seed beds as inevitably as motorists seeking roadside facilities and birds will bathe in any dustiness with the avidity of tired footballers in their post-match tub. Slugs, vexed by the general scratchiness of the surrounding soil, will congregate on its easeful surface, there to find not only comfortable, frequently watered lodging, but an excellent restaurant as well.

Against cat damage, there are plastic devices available which lodge into the soil and have short, upward-pointing spokes – a bit like a crown of thorns – and are useful for flower borders. For vegetables, you can use horticultural fleece. If you don't object to using chemicals against slugs, water with liquid slug killer.

VEGETABLES

All of the advice on sowing annuals applies to vegetable seeds too but in general the conditions do not need to be quite as perfect. Of course, you must ensure there are no perennial weeds where you sow the seeds, but the seedlings are usually so much more robust and quick into growth that annual weeds are not that much of a problem. Vegetables are usually sown in rows, labelled of course, and you will soon find yourself in a routine of hoeing between rows to keep the weeds down while the plants are still very young.

If you like to have your rows of vegetables in apple-pie order, with no gaps where there have been failures, sow a few spares at the ends of the rows, particularly with peas and beans. You can then transplant them into the gaps as long as you do it early enough. With seeds such as parsnips that are generally poor germinators, sow three seeds at each station and thin them down as necessary.

SPECIAL TREATMENT

Don't forget that vegetables, like other plants, divide themselves into cool-country and warm-country plants. You will not have much success with cucurbits (marrows, ridge cucumbers, courgettes and so on) if you sow them out of doors. They are best sown individually in pots in a cold frame or in gentle heat.

Modular sowing, in which seeds are sown in small individual pots, is an excellent way of giving many vegetables a flying start, especially those that are tender and cannot safely be sown outside until mid-summer. Chinese radish, for example, can be sown in modules in early summer and planted out already in growth when outdoor sowings would only just be beginning.

On the whole, if you decide to confine your outdoor sowings to vegetables, you will be in line with a majority of gardeners. If you include hardy annuals in your plans you will still be in a majority, but a smaller one.

Modular sowing is really a fancy way of referring to sowing seeds in individual pots.

TREES AND SHRUBS

Tree and shrub seeds grown in the open are a great deal of trouble. In forestry nurseries, where large quantities are sown in long rows, a proportion of losses is acceptable. If a mouse comes along and eats six acorns out of a couple of hundred, there is little harm done. On the other hand, if he visits your garden and in order to satisfy his hunger takes all six of the acorns you have sown it is another matter altogether. Mice, squirrels, birds and weeds seem like divisions within a mighty army whereas there is only one of you.

Furthermore, it is much easier if you deal with as many of your seeds as possible in the shelter of your potting shed and with your back in comfortable lordosis (its correct position – not the slumped one you are sitting in now). Take no notice of those who say that some trees and shrubs simply must be sown where they are to grow because they hate root disturbance. Sow them one seed to a pot – or two and eliminate one of the resulting seedlings – and plant them out before the roots start to curl around the pots. If it is ever necessary to do something to plants that they do not like, the thing is to do it in a manner that prevents them from noticing.

TREES FROM SEED

Or is it worth it?

Much of what you can read about growing trees from seed comes from the pens of foresters, who are used to working in hundreds if not thousands of acres and who grow trees on a large scale.

Forestry techniques are not really relevant to home gardeners. As we have seen, sowing in outdoor seed beds, essential for the production of large numbers, is neither necessary nor particularly desirable. Coming right down to the other end of the scale – to someone with room only for one or two trees – is it worth growing them from seed? In general, it is probably not, though there are several factors to consider first.

WHAT TO TAKE INTO ACCOUNT

HOW MANY?

When you have room for more than the half dozen or so that will define your garden in its initial stages, you can then certainly think in terms of growing fom seed. After all, trees involve quite an outlay when bought as anything more than very small, feathered specimens. Furthermore, there are some delightful trees that are not so easy to obtain but whose seed might come your way.

HOW LONG WILL THEY TAKE TO GROW?

People quite often say that it is not worth growing trees from seed because it takes such a long time for them to reach any

How do you collect seed of a large tree?

This is a question that vexes people. Answer: collect it on the ground. But what if there's a lot of undergrowth, herbaceous perennials etc.? Answer: mow, cut back, or spread and peg plastic sheets to catch the seed.

meaningful size. There is a certain amount of truth in that, but it is also true that a tree, well grown from seed without a check or any pot-binding, will swiftly outgrow one a few years older that has perhaps not had the best of care and has stood around in the nursery or in the garden centre row for rather too long.

Then again, some trees are remarkably fast-growing. I once raised a tree of the florists' mimosa (*Acacia dealbata*) from seed to approximately 12m (40ft) high in nine years. Eucalyptus grow very fast, too, and are much better if planted in mid-summer of the same year in which they were sown in late winter. They should be neither manured nor staked and will grow arrow-straight and astonishingly quickly. Bought in a nursery or garden centre (and sold, I may say, in perfectly good faith) at about 1.5m (5ft) high and staked, they will fall over as soon as the stake is removed, no matter how long it is left on. You then have to cut them to ground level and when, as they usually do, new shoots grow from the base, you choose one and hope that it will grow nice and straight as a replacement main stem. Meanwhile, your seedling has raced away like the tree version of a Ferrari.

It is not only more or less tender trees such as these that are fast-growing. *Acer pensylvanicum*, a lovely snake-bark maple with butter-yellow autumn leaves, will be a significant element in the garden after about seven years. Another maple, *Acer flabellatum* var. *yunnanense* can put on well over 60cm (2ft) in height a year while it is young. Both are hardy trees and they are by no means exceptional.

EXPERIMENTAL TREATMENT OF SEED

Although I give you the counsel of perfection in the lists in Chapter 14, please don't be afraid to split batches of seed and try

The male catkins
(left) of the silver
birch (Betula pen-
dula) appear in
spring, but the female
ones (right) elongate
in autumn and break
up into individual
seeds.

Pere David's or
snake-bark maple
(Acer davidii) shows
a completely different
kind of seed – a
winged seed, or
samara, designed to
ensure it is carried
some distance from
the parent.

something different. To give you an example, I once received seed of the canoe birch, *Betula papyrifera*, from Warren County, New York, and split the batch into two halves, to one of which I gave the alternate chilling/warming treatment. I saved the other for sowing directly in spring. Both batches germinated extremely well. The following year I received seed of the same species from the same source and again treated the two batches differently. This time the pre-chilled seed came up like cress, while from the spring-sown batch there emerged just two seedlings.

Authoritative sources will tell you that *Sophora tetraptera*, a most beautiful tree from New Zealand with bright yellow, pea-type flowers in big clusters, must have its seed soaked in boiling water or be subject to abrasion if it is to germinate at all. I was sent an enormous amount of seed one year from two wild stands in New Zealand and set up an experiment.

From each stand, 150 seeds were split into 50s, one of which was treated with boiling water, one with abrasion, and to the last nothing was done at all. The 300 seeds were sown on the same day in the same kind of compost and placed in the same frame. Germination occurred after five weeks and was complete after seven. The germination rate was between 43 and 48 out of 50 in every one of the six batches. There was no difference at all. This does not prove anything very much except the very important fact that nothing in nature is carved in tablets of stone. If some gardening guru says 'Thou shalt not …' it is time to do it and try to prove him or her wrong. The thing is, however, to do it with only half or less of your plant material. The same goes with 'Thou shalt …' but perhaps even more so.

HOW HARDY WILL THEY BE?

Pronouncements about the hardiness of many kinds of plants, but particularly some trees, are reliable only if their provenance (i.e. where they come from) is taken into account. If you are not familiar with this term, it is probably best explained by an example.

The Sitka spruce grows wild from northern California, through British Columbia, up to Alaska. There is a considerable difference in climate between the two extremes of its range, with a gradient in between. In British Columbia the climate is similar to that of western Britain. Seed from trees native to British Columbia produces, in western parts of the British Isles, the fastest rate of timber production of all trees and complete resistance to salty gales. Alaskan seeds make for trees that are much slower-growing because in Britain they lack the long, Arctic summer days. Trees of Californian provenance grow slowly too, as they do not receive adequate warmth.

The number of species of *Eucalyptus* that can be grown well in England has increased in recent years from two or three to a dozen or more because of exploitation of seed from the highest altitudes and most southerly latitudes where the species grow. Many species range over wide variations in altitude, with specimens at low levels never experiencing frosts while those from the mountains suffer them every winter. Cold-provenance seeds produce trees that survive the English winter, while those from warmer provenances do not.

It is mistake to think that plant species adapt so that each generation is hardier than the next. What can happen, though, is that only the hardiest cultivated trees will survive in gardens near to their climatic limit long enough to set seed themselves.

Tree and shrub nurserymen will often try to obtain seed of species from the provenances that come nearest to the climate of the country or countries that constitute their main markets. It is in their commercial interest to do so but it is also very much to our advantage as well.

WHAT COULD IT COST?

One of the great advantages of growing from seed is that the risk you take in trying species that are only marginally hardy in your area is small. You would think twice about investing a substantial sum in such a tree as a bought-in specimen, whereas the outlay on seed can be from nothing at all to just a few coins. Furthermore, you are likely to be able to raise a few plants, so that you can try them in different parts of the garden where there are likely to be different micro-climates.

You may also be able to save a plant or two as a replacement in case of loss, and if your source of seed is a fairly constant one, you can sow a batch every couple of years or so. It is by growing tenderish plant species from seed that gardeners manage to establish them, much more readily than by buying specimens from nurseries.

What do you want from trees?

Trees can offer: beautiful bark; attractive foliage; colour in branches and twigs; flowers; fruits; berries; autumn colour.

WHAT WILL THEY CONTRIBUTE TO THE GARDEN?

If you are going to grow trees in your garden it is a very good thing to be as sure as you can that each one will contribute all year round. There are so many tree species that combine beautiful bark, lovely foliage sometimes with good autumn colour, significant flowers and long-lasting, colourful fruits and berries that it is a waste of valuable space to grow any that perform poorly by comparison. I would not, for example, grow an alder where a Japanese maple could take its place, nor a common sallow where a willow with blue, red or yellow branches and twigs would put on a much better show. White-barked birches, mountain ashes with long-lasting berries such as *Sorbus vilmorinii* and eucalyptus, whose evergreen foliage, often blue or blue-grey, is a delight every month of the year, are the sorts of trees that are worth the trouble of raising and the space they will occupy.

So yes, it really is worth growing trees from seed. The bigger your garden the more worthwhile it becomes, but in even the smallest you can enjoy the experience of looking at a beautiful tree that was once a seed betweeen your fingers. What is more, you can enjoy it every day, and for a long succession of days at that. Chapter 14 gives details of some you could try.

9

SHRUBS FROM SEED

Or one for sorrow, two for joy

THE USEFULNESS OF SHRUBS

Shrubs are the main stock in trade, as far as plants go, of nurseries and garden centres. They make good, saleable plants quickly and command high prices. There is a wide variety of shrubs that are easy to grow in almost any soil and in most climates. They are long-term fixtures in the garden and suppress weeds. They need no staking and you do not have to go over the whole lot cutting them back or lifting and dividing, as with herbaceous perennials. A little judicious pruning here and there, a fairly casual watch for pests and diseases and you have low-maintenance gardening.

So what is against the idea of going to a garden centre and buying all your shrubs? Well, a lot of people do but they are likely in the end to find themselves growing much the same as everyone else in the area while having spent a lot of money. Off-the-shelf gardening is an expensive business.

If you are a seed-raising gardener you will want something different. You will be on the look-out for the unusual and the unexpected. You should certainly buy or at least grow from cuttings all those shrubs that are garden varieties (cultivars), as they are clones and will not come anything like true from seed, but there is an enormous selection of species shrubs that can be grown highly economically from seed.

Furthermore, most of us tend to buy just one specimen of each shrub. This lends a spotty appearance to the garden and, even in a small space, it is good sometimes to alleviate this effect with a grouping of just one kind. In a larger garden you can plant several groups and even make a feature of a group of something like *Rhododendron luteum*, the scented, yellow-flowered deciduous azalea whose autumn foliage is ravishingly crimson, orange and purple. When you first see its tiny seedlings you may wonder if you will live to see the show, but good cultivation will bring results in a surprisingly low number of years. Sow it in spring (it is difficult to over-winter autumn seedlings) on the surface of a peat-based compost with no added lime – often called an ericaceous compost.

WHICH SHRUBS FROM SEED?

Many tender or marginally tender shrubs and shrubs that have only recently been introduced to cultivation are ideally grown from seed, certainly when they are new to you. Later on, you should be able to grow them from cuttings, but initially you are more than likely to find they come your way in the form of seed.

This is because shrubs that are slightly tender are not a good risk for garden centres. If they are recognizably conservatory or greenhouse subjects, well and good; they will be sold as such in the appropriate department but, if they are not, the business faces the risk on the one hand of losing the plants to the cold and on the other of not convincing the public that they are worth spending money on.

Recent introductions are most unlikely to arrive in commerce until they have been tried, tested and propagated in large quantities. Seed tends to circulate privately among keen gardeners and you may be given some at your garden club or find it in a specialist list, perhaps even that of a botanic garden. Then again, many new introductions never make it as nurserymen's plants because they are perhaps very slow to grow or rather difficult for one reason or another. Perhaps, too, they are hard to strike as cuttings and set only a small amount of seed. Even such as thing as a cumbersome, long Latin name could be enough to ensure that a good shrub is a failure in the marketplace.

Once a really superior form of a shrub has been isolated from the general run of seedlings and named, you should not sow its seeds. It should thereafter be grown as a clonal cultivar and be propagated by cuttings, layers or other vegetative means. We have already looked at this in a previous chapter (see page 51) but it is often not realized that a cultivar name is frequently given to forms with larger flowers than usual or to individuals that are more free-flowering than the general run of seedlings. A fancy name does not necessarily indicate a different colour, double flowers, or something as dramatically different as any cultivar of *Camellia japonica* is from the true species.

The sweet pepper bush, *Clethra alnifolia*, has scented, white flowers in racemes. A raceme is a simple, straight flower cluster (inflorescence) with each flower on its own stalk along the axis. However, *C.a.* 'Paniculata' has its flowers in panicles, in which the flower stalks are themselves racemes, and it is a much more effective plant. Sow seed of it, though, and it is very unlikely indeed that the seedlings will have anything like the flower power of 'Paniculata'. Therefore, it should be propagated by cuttings.

There are traps for the unwary, but life's like that. *Carpenteria californica*, sometimes known as tree anemone, has large, white flowers in the middle of summer if it has a warm, sunny spot in

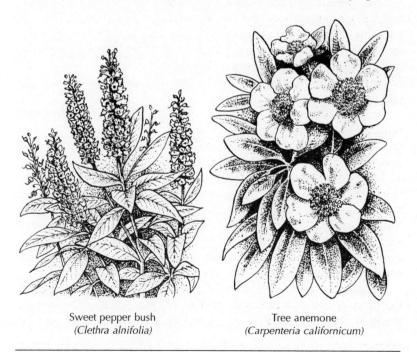

Sweet pepper bush
(*Clethra alnifolia*)

Tree anemone
(*Carpenteria californicum*)

which to grow. How large they are is another matter. Two forms, 'Ladham's Variety' and 'Bodnant' have been raised which have even larger flowers than unnamed forms and should always be propagated vegetatively. However, specimens sold simply under the species name usually have very good flowers, if not quite as big as the two named ones. This position is under threat because in fact all the original introductions to cultivation had unusually large flowers compared to the run of those in the wild, and were the result of selections from the wild population in western North America. If you sow seed, you will end up with plants that are very inferior to any you might buy, although, sad to say, there are now some poor plants creeping onto the market.

COLLECTORS' NUMBERS

Nevertheless, as time goes on you will soon work your way into sowing shrubs that are really worth it and leaving alone the ones that are not. Among them there may be some with collectors' numbers, which may turn out to be the best of the lot or could be hopeless as garden plants. This is where, as a seed-raiser, you can play a part in the advancement of horticulture.

Collectors, often academic horticulturists or botanists but equally often practising professional gardeners, sometimes full-time professional collectors, and even highly talented and knowledgeable amateurs, mount expeditions to distant countries in order to collect seed of garden-worthy plants. Unless you are one such person, please leave all wild plants alone wherever you are. Meanwhile, you can benefit from the work of people who may have spent a great deal of time and effort in obtaining the necessary permissions or licences to make official botanical collections.

They send shares of seed to the subscribers to their expeditions. Each batch will be numbered, usually with a set of letters followed by numbers. For example. SBEC stands for the Sino-British Expedition to the Cang-Shan (a range of mountains in Yunnan Province, China); L stands for Roy Lancaster, SSW for Stainton, Sykes and Williams – and so on. Suppose I collected seed from a particularly fine specimen of *Rara ultima* and gave it the number JK

65, you should keep that number with your share of that seed for the whole of the life of the plant. No other collectings of *Rara ultima* would carry that number, and JK 64 and 66 could be quite different forms of the same species or from a different sort of habitat.

If you grow seed from collectors' numbers, you may one day find yourself the only possessor of a cultivated specimen of some great rarity from a country whose wild habitats are closed for political reasons. It may be decades before it is likely to be collected again. Habitats are destroyed daily by human's so-called progress – which is usually only another way of describing over-population of the planet – and not only in the tropical rain forests. One collector told me that he once stood in the precise spot from which a predecessor had taken a photograph of the hills in the middle distance some half a century earlier. Then they had been covered in rhododendron and azalea scrub in which lurked some of the most delectable treasures of our gardens and a wealth of nature's most beautiful plants. As he stood there with the old photograph in his hand he looked up and saw ... nothing. Bare, brown hills stretched away into the distance. Every twig, stick and root had gone to the cooking fires of the local people.

Gardening is not simply a matter of making pleasant places in which to live. It is not even confined to creating beauty and gaining deep emotional satisfaction. It also has to do with conserving nature's species when they are threatened with extinction. To concern oneself exclusively with the 'wildflowers' of one's immediate land is to be incredibly blinkered. We belong to the world, it is the world that is suffering, and we can help in our small ways on a wider canvas more than we are sometimes encouraged to imagine.

Growing woody species – trees and shrubs – from seed is much more important an activity than most people realize. If you haven't tried it so far, are you ready to begin? Then see Chapter 14.

10

PERENNIALS FROM SEED

Or bordering on the inexpensive

HERBACEOUS PLANTS

The whole question of what is a herbaceous plant is as vexed as the definition of a perennial. As with, for example, 'cultivar', 'herbaceous' is a precise term that has acquired a jargon meaning among gardeners. Strictly speaking, it is simply a plant that is green, soft-textured and non-woody, but is often defined as a non-woody plant that loses its above-ground parts for the winter and re-emerges in spring. The plant may be annual, perennial or biennial, but we use the term exclusively in gardening for perennials.

PERENNIAL BORDERS

I have never quite grown an entire herbaceous border from seed. This is partly because I have never been able to exclude a few shrubs and roses and also because I like to grow named cultivars of delphiniums and one or two other plants that must be propagated from cuttings or division. I enjoy, too, growing long-flowering tender perennials such as *Argyranthemum* 'Jamaica Primrose' and clonal cultivars of *Osteospermum*, which need to have cuttings taken every year as the plants are frequently lost in winter.

This does not mean it is impossible. On the contrary, it would be a most exciting thing to do and one day I will. Meanwhile, why

Leave seed - heads on

Many people don't grow perennials from seed because they think they should 'cut back' in autumn. In fact seed heads and stems are attractive winter decoration and can be left. Whatever seed is required can be harvested when ready.

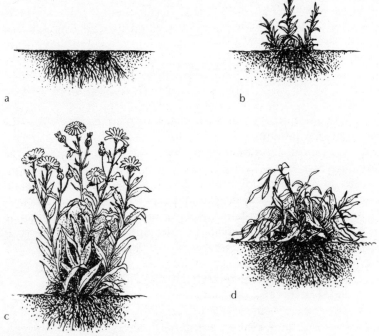

Yearly cycle of a herbaceous perennial:
(a) In winter nothing shows above ground and the plant is dormant, although some development of roots and crowns will slowly take place when the soil temperature is above 5˚C/41˚F.
(b) Spring sees the vigorous development of new shoots.
(c) Many of the new shoots elongate in late spring, summer or autumn into flowering stems.
(d) In late autumn the stems fall or are cut down, leaving the leafy shoots to manufacture food before they too wither in preparation for winter.

don't you try it? Many people think that the result will be about as dramatic as one of those wildflower borders but it will in fact be practically indistinguishable from a border made up entirely of named garden varieties.

I moved house some years ago and inherited a border about 35m (40yd) long by an average of 3.5m (4yd) wide. That is quite a large area of garden and I wanted to fill it with herbaceous perennials, bulbs and some ferns. The sheer cost of buying in the perennials was terrifying. Even growing just one or two of a kind and then waiting three years until I could divide them would still have left me with a big bill for plants. I decided instead to grow the majority from seed. Within three years I had a lovely border with groupings of fascinating plants, many of which I had not seen before, let alone grown. The few shrubs and three trees had their feet awash in colour for months on end. While admittedly the last colour of the year was from *Argyranthemum* 'Jamaica Primrose' grown from cuttings, the greater part by far of the display was from seed-raised plants.

The great majority of seed-raised perennials can thereafter be propagated by vegetative means, but not all. Hollyhocks, for instance, are much better raised from seed every year. As perennials they are shortlived and become prone to rust disease, but during the first flowering (second) season they are magnificent, person-high plants. The 'Chater's' varieties are perhaps the best and include 'Chater's Double Apricot', in which completely double, ruffled flowers in shades that harmonize with just about everything else clothe almost the entire lengths of the stems.

PERENNIALS NEED TIME

Most perennials take a year in which to build themselves up before doing much in the way of flowering, and it is in fact best to remove any flower stems that appear during the first season. There is often a surprising difference between the appearance of a plant as it dies down for its first winter and its strength, vigour and proliferation of foliage when it emerges in the spring. To let it flower may well tax it so much that it cannot manage this and fails to make it into its second year. This is particularly important with the Himalayan blue poppies (*Meconopsis*). These wonderful plants, which make a display unrivalled for elegance and provide an element of the

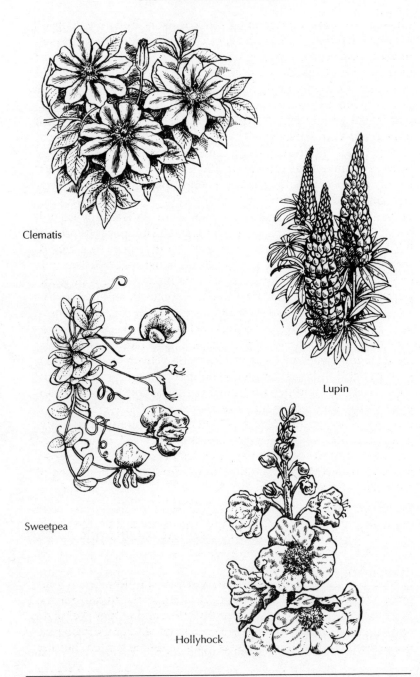

Clematis

Lupin

Sweetpea

Hollyhock

unusual in a moisture-retaining soil, consist of true perennials on the one hand and monocarpic species that die after their first setting of seed on the other. If you allow the perennials, the most well known of which is *M. betonicifolia*, to flower in their first year, they are highly likely to turn monocarpic. If you remove the flower stems before they are too advanced, the energies of the plants will go into growth instead and you will encourage them to perform as true perennials.

If you can obtain seed of *Meconopsis grandis*, which has huge flowers of the purest blue up to 12cm (5in) across on 60cm (2ft) stems, it is worth taking every precaution and using all your self-discipline to see that they become a long-term feature of your garden and not just a one-year wonder. The flowers will be much better, too. It is one of the scarcer blue poppies offered by Thompson & Morgan, who also reintroduced the monocarpic, yellow-flowered *M. regia* to their list in 1996. This one should be allowed to flower as soon as it shows signs of wanting to, although you may find that it waits until its second year.

Dianthus – the pinks and carnations but not of course the annuals – are among herbaceous plants such as bergenias and phormiums that can be termed evergreen perennials. You can raise the most magnificent show of border carnations from seed, including such delightful dwarf strains as 'Lillipot' that grow to less than 30cm (1ft) high and need no pinching out. Pinks provide cushions of grey, grey-green, blue-green or silvery foliage throughout the year. I have grown *Dianthus* 'Allwoodii Alpinus' most of my gardening life and have always looked forward to the subtle variations in flowers and foliage that result from a generous sowing. They can be tried as edging, in the front of the border or, of course, on the rock garden.

PLANNING A PERENNIAL BORDER

A good border is always planned, and you should prepare your order for seeds with this in mind. It is a mistake to aim for too long a season, as this leads to a spotty effect and to there being no real show at any particular time. When to have your main display is a matter of taste and what else is going on in the garden, but my

When planning a border

Consider:
◆ Which time of year do you want the fullest display?
◆ A theme of colour, or choosing a succession of dominant plants, often works better than trying for a bit of everything. Colour themeing uses one main colour and its shades to dominate a border, but doesn't exclude using other colours.
◆ In a small garden, a wide, deep border has more impact than a long, narrow one.

own inclination is to make much of June, which is a month in which the shrubs are doing very little, and late summer, perhaps late enough to be centred around Michaelmas daisies.

In early summer, lupins, pinks, delphiniums and oriental poppies take the stage, striking a cottagey note and contrasting delightfully with the burgeoning foliage of the plants that are to flower later. I do, as I said earlier, like to grow named, vegetatively propagated cultivars of delphiniums, but they are not always very easy to obtain and you can raise some very fine ones from seed. 'Southern Jesters' and 'Southern Noblemen' are alternatives to the well known 'Pacific Giant' mixed strain, and, if you want something shorter in the stem, 'Dwarf Blue Heaven' and 'Dwarf Snowwhite', at less than 90cm (3ft) will fit into the smallest border.

The chief reason for my growing the delphiniums I choose is because I plant them in clumps at very regular spacing in the border – sometimes white, light blue and dark blue in a repeated pattern but by no means always boringly the same – to provide order and a central motif to the border in early and mid-summer. It is all too easy for a predominantly seed-raised border to become a mess in terms of design, and I come back to the planning that really should accompany your decision to go in for perennials from seed.

You should always try to avoid the patchwork-quilt type of planting. It is often advocated, but rarely works. It is much better to take a theme either of colour or of a succession of dominant plants. For a season with two high points, delphiniums and Michaelmas daisies can be the major elements – lupins instead of delphiniums if you want the first pulse to be even earlier – or you could provide succession with lupins, delphiniums, and then phloxes, with Michaelmas daises heralding autumn. It all boils down to how much room you have. With a small border it is best to go for two main flushes of flowering, whereas with a larger one you can aim for three or even four. Complete continuity is the counsel of perfection but it simply never happens – at least, not without a lot of work involving lifting plants and inserting others that have been grown in pots, which is how it is often done professionally.

COLOUR PLANNING

Colour co-ordination is a fashionable trend that involves toning everything into a colour theme – bronze, perhaps, or yellow (a favourite). Colour theming on the other hand is the practice of using one colour and its shades to dominate a border without excluding other colours. Thus a border might have one third dominated by yellow, another by white, and a third by shades of pink – or may contain a main feature whose colour is repeated at intervals as echoes among other colours.

What is hard to do, unless you are an artist or have unusually acute colour sense, is to create a border in which colours shade and blend one into another in a progression. It is especially difficult if you are growing plants from seed, as nuances of colour are difficult to predict. On the other hand, you will know whether a batch of seed is likely to produce flowers within the range you are looking for, and you can choose accordingly, building up a population for the area you have designated for that particular theme.

PLANNING SIZE AND SHAPE

Try if you can to make your border as wide as possible. Most herbaceous borders lack impact because they are too narrow and the eye has to make a long sweep to be much affected. In a small garden it is often better to make a square or broad oblong rather than the usual long shape. It is, of course, perfectly good gardening practice to mix annuals with perennials and they are often the real key to whatever degree of continuity a smaller garden – or even a larger one – can provide.

11

ANNUALS FROM SEED

Or painting by catalogue numbers

ANNUALS BOUGHT AS BEDDING PLANTS

There are all sorts of reasons for sowing your own annuals rather than buying them as plants in trays. For instance, growers like to produce varieties that remain short enough so that when the trays are stacked they are not in the least squashed. They always go for the earliest to flower, too, as these are what sell on the mass market. It seems that people just can't convince themselves soon enough that summer has arrived. Commercial growers also have an entirely understandable preference for producing plants in flower – after all, if a tray of bedding plants is to sell, will it do so quicker with colour showing or without?

THE VALUE OF GROWING FROM SEED

HALF-HARDY AND HARDY ANNUALS

Before we do anything else, perhaps it would be a good idea to sort out the terms 'hardy' and 'half-hardy' as they apply to annuals.

An annual is a plant that naturally germinates, sets seed and dies all in the same year. A half-hardy annual is one that will not stand the cold in a given climate zone and thus cannot be sown before all danger of frost is over. A hardy annual is one that will stand frost in the climate zone in which it grows. It depends on the depth of frost. In Britain, for example, any degree of frost and even prolonged temperatures below 5°C (41°F) will kill many plants such as busy lizzies. These are therefore regarded as half-hardy annuals even though they are perennials in nature and even in sub-tropical places where frosts occur but are very shortlived and alternate with relatively high temperatures.

If you grow your own – and I am largely talking of the advantages with half-hardy annuals – you needn't stick to the low, cushiony sorts that never move or sway in the most vigorous breeze. You can grow taller plants that have rather more character and among these are several that are excellent for cutting. *Dianthus chinensis* 'Black and White Minstrels', for example, is a half-hardy annual growing to about 35cm (14in) that you are highly unlikely to find in the garden centre, and the brightly coloured, scented flowers are long-lasting and summery indoors in a vase. Of course, you can grow a wide range of hardy annuals as cut flowers, none perhaps more exciting than the newer sunflower introductions such as 'Prado Red', 'Prado Yellow' and the mixed 'Pastiche', all of which score by having short stems for sunflowers and very little pollen to stain your clothes or furnishings.

You will not feel the need to sow the earliest bloomers, largely because you will not want to waste your efforts in raising them by putting them out when there is a risk of losing them to frost. Furthermore, you will find that the great majority of half-hardy annuals plant out best when they are still all green and showing no flower buds. They still have time to put their energies into making good root systems before being diverted into flower production.

Annuals are best thought of as adjuncts to more permanent plantings. The plants that grow and mature year after year give character to the garden; annuals are embellishments. When I bought my first house, which was in the north of England a very long time ago, one of my next-door neighbours was an avid gardener with half-hardy annuals. His garden was a picture from late spring to early autumn and bare soil for the rest of the year. The picture was, however, a static one, rather as if the ground had been painted. There were mesembryanthemums precisely *so*, blue lobelias alternating with white alyssum exactly along *there*, short gazanias just *here* – and so forth. I have never seen such perfection before or since but it was, unfortunately, also a most boring garden.

HALF-HARDY ANNUALS AS SPACE-FILLERS

The best approach nowadays is not to assume that painting on a bare canvas is all the use to which annuals can be put. They are indeed very much more versatile than that. One of the very best ways of using half-hardy annuals is to fill in the inevitable gaps that occur in your mixed borders. Oh, you don't have any? Well, in that case your borders must be singularly unadventurous, because mine do, I can assure you.

When the spring daffodils finish flowering, their leaves must be left alone for seven weeks, otherwise you won't have any flowers the following year. Busy lizzies are the ideal plants to put among the leaves, as they are attractive from the day in late spring when you plant them out to the frosts, long before which they will have grown together and completely covered the soil where the bulbs are then enjoying the coolness they provide. Don't do this with tulips as they need all the sun that's going when they are dormant.

If I have a gap caused by a shrub's having had to be moved, or perhaps it has died, or maybe I just miscalculated and left a space, I plant *Nicotiana* 'Lime Green'. The tobacco plants are lovely – anything from 25cm (10 in) to the 75cm (30in) of 'Lime Green'. Patches of them here and there lend elegance and beauty as well as scent, but 'Lime Green' is in a class of its own, as its colour goes with everything and clashes with nothing – it is a sort of universal donor among plants.

CHOOSING ANNUALS FOR COLOUR

The ground-painting, painstaking pattern-making of the traditional gardeners with annuals, who often – but not always – fell into the most dreadful disharmonies with colour, is fast becoming a thing of the past. Competitions are still won, however, by such gardens and I shall never forget attempting to get permission to take photographs of perhaps the most startling garden I had ever seen (it was in Ireland) and being threatened for my pains with having the dogs set on me. Perhaps the owner thought I wanted to use the pictures to write a snobbish, mickey-taking article, but I would never do that.

The reason why I would not do so is because there is no room for such attitudes in gardening. What gives a gardener pleasure is their affair, and if it pleases others enough for them to award prizes, who am I to stand in judgement? And yet people do. They sneer at annuals and consider them to be below the attention of expert, knowledgable, proper gardeners who talk about how well such and such a rarity does 'with me'.

Would that they would glance through modern seed catalogues and, converted, allow themselves to raise a few trays of some of the annuals available today that appeal to the most demanding plantsmanlike gardener (a term which applies equally to men and women). Modern mixtures of *Phlox drummondii* are as elegant as any perennials and hardly at fault for lasting but a season. How many have lost perennial phloxes to eelworm and not been able to grow them again? And how can anyone dismiss godetias, of which a drift of one colour, sown in the open where it is to make its display, can be the most heavenly counterpoint to a tall perennial and will flower on as a complementary or contrasting echo after it has finished?

Admittedly, plantsmanlike people prefer longer-lived plants that have qualities other than flowers – interesting foliage, elegant habit and so on. But the same is true of so many annuals, especially those which are in truth perennials but cannot stand our winters. *Linum grandiflorum album*, for example, has all the elegance for which you could wish, with a perfect balance of cool, white flowers and fresh, green foliage. No better or more aristocratic plant could be called on to take part in the border pageant. There are some more frequently used hardy plants which, it has to be said, would fall far short of its many weeks of flowering.

Then some would say that annuals are a great deal of trouble, having to be raised from seed every year. And yet they may take infinitely more pains in raising cuttings of other sorts of plants. Those who might scorn growing half-hardy annuals nevertheless revel in osteospermums, argyranthemums and other tender perennials, taking cuttings of them every late summer lest they be lost in winter – as they frequently are. It is little trouble to put pots or trays on a well-lit windowsill. Even better is a propagator large enough to take a few pots and capable of maintaining a temperature of 24°C (75°F). It is surely no further trouble to wait for two to three weeks until germination takes place. One hour

The kitchen windowsill is traditionally the site of much success in seed-raising, but there are extra precautions to be taken. Turn the pots once or twice daily so that the seedlings do not reach for the light, and place them so that they are on the room side of the blind or curtain, otherwise they will be badly chilled at night.

is long enough to prick out a very large number, and hardening-off is no great problem. The results in terms of joyous colour are unmatchable and, in terms of finance, unbeatable.

Although I recommend using clingfilm to assist in germinating several types of seeds that need very high, consistent humidity, the laboratory boffins prefer polybags, as they make more air available to the seeds. They are of course right, but clingfilm is neater, takes up less room (which is important for home gardeners) and is all right providing you remove it every few days to allow fresh air in. Turn the clingfilm as you do so.

PLANNING FOR COLOUR HARMONY

It is not merely as adjuncts to the perennial features of the garden that annuals should be used. While it is highly desirable to avoid ground-painting and essential to the sanity of everyone to make sure nothing happens like the traffic-circle planting of certain sea-side resort towns in the south of England (where things are done with African marigolds that should qualify as vandalism) planting systems using annuals alone can be entirely bewitching.

The secret lies in understatement. If you allow each distinct group of annuals to make itself felt and avoid over-facing the onlooker, using perhaps green foliage or grey paving to act as foils for the bright colours – or if you contrast quiet, neutral colours with the stronger ones, and if you resist at all costs any smallest move towards loudness or discordant colour combinations, you will be able to create a garden as good as anyone's. There is a good deal to be said for using annuals exclusively in tiny city gardens, which can look dreadfully tatty in winter and are perhaps best reduced to the bones of their structure once the frosts, rain and general muck take over. One of the best gardens I have ever seen, and one that caused me to leave a streak of rubber on the road as it caught my eye as I drove past, was a very small, entirely modest yard in Berkshire with paving, a few urns and a theme of deep blush-red and warm pink, all done with annuals and with great use made of contrasting flower shapes and variations in height. To my great regret nobody was in and I could not tell them how much I liked it.

BIENNIALS

Biennials are plants that do their growing in their first season; flowering, setting seed and dying in their second.

Sow in drills from early to late summer and shade lightly until germination is complete. The summer sun is an enemy because of dryness, so the bed should preferably face west or east. Transplant into rows 25cm (10in) apart when large enough to handle. Final transplanting to where they are to flower is done in autumn, but for summer-flowering biennials in cold areas spring may be better.

Among biennials are *Campanula medium* (Canterbury bells), *Dianthus barbatus* (Sweet William), *Lunaria annua* (honesty), *Papaver nudicaule* (Iceland poppy), monocarpic meconopsis, stocks and wallflowers.

SOWING AND GROWING:
A SELECTION OF ANNUALS

The great majority of annuals will germinate well if you use the methods I have suggestedor half-hardy annuals under cover and hardy ones out of doors (page 71).

It would really be quite impossible to list all the annuals and give detailed instructions for each one. However, the following are some that are not so easy and which have given gardeners trouble in the past. You should succeed if you follow the suggestions given for each.

Geraniums
Half-hardy perennials treated as half-hardy annuals.

Geranium is the genus to which the hardy cranesbills belong, but the name is commonly used for zonal pelargoniums, and it is these that present difficulties for many gardeners. When you have spent £3 or $5 or so for half a dozen seeds of an F_1 hybrid, you want to make sure you get a result.

Sowing is best done in mid-winter. You should use a small pot and space the seeds out evenly, sowing each individually. Cover with a very thin layer of compost and water with a fine rose or even a mist spray, but make sure there is no dry compost left.

Wrap the pot in clingfilm drawn tight over its top or in a secured plastic bag . Place the pot in a propagator set to 21–24°C (70–75°F).

Seedlings may emerge in as little as three or as many as 21 days as long as there is constant moisture but not a state of waterlogging.

As soon as the seedlings can be handled, prick them out (see page 66) into 7.5cm (3in) pots and keep the temperature at 18°C (65°F) at night and 21°C (70°F) by day. Gradually reduce the night temperature to 13–15°C (55–60°F) over a period of six weeks or so, but try not to let it fall further as development of the plants is then slowed down. Treated in this way, seed should produce flowers by late spring.

Busy Lizzie
(Impatiens)
Half-hardy perennials
treated as half-hardy
annuals.

The critical factors with busy lizzies are light, temperature and humidity. Most gardeners find them difficult, or at least reluctant to germinate freely.

First, sow the seed in spring on the surface of the compost and do not cover it at all. The compost should be evenly moist and not waterlogged.

As with geraniums, wrap the pot in clingfilm drawn tight over the top. This will keep the moisture constant and will maintain high humidity. Keep the temperature above 21°C (70°F) night and day in a propagator, lowering it after germination to 18°C (65°F).

Begonias
Half-hardy perennials
treated as half-hardy
annuals.

Begonia seed is dust-fine and its embryos are almost unprotected and are damaged by rough or careless handling. Sow them in the same way as busy lizzies but give early sowings eight hours of supplementary lighting a day, using a fluorescent tube. You should expect germination in about one month. If you cannot provide the extra lighting, postpone sowing until late winter.

Bells of Ireland
(Moluccella laevis)
Technically a hardy
annual, but best
treated as half-hardy.

Outdoor sowing of this extremely long-lasting, flower arranger's plant is highly unsatisfactory. Sow the seeds so that they are covered with their own depth of compost and wrap the pot in clingfilm to maintain the moisture. Put the pot in the fridge for 14 days and then place it in a propagator set to 21°C (70°F) or a little lower. Germination should be complete in about one month. Prick the seedlings out into individual pots and keep on thinking of them as half-hardy annuals.

Basket campanulas
(Campanula
isophylla)
Half-hardy perennial
treated as half-hardy
annual.

Several factors have usually defeated those trying to germinate the very fine seed of this species. First, the seed must not be covered at all. Second, there must be constant humidity round the seeds, and this is achieved by wrapping the pot in clingfilm. Third, high temperatures inhibit germination and so do fluctuating ones: the secret is to keep the thermometer at 15°C (60°F) and, fourth, if you don't lower the humidity when germination is under way, the seedlings will rot off – so take the clingfilm away as soon as you see a good crop of seedlings. It is also a bad mistake to sow other than thinly.

Black-eyed Susan
(Thunbergia)
Half-hardy or green-
house annual.

Treat as busy lizzies but cover the seeds with their own depth of compost.

Coleus
Half-hardy perennial
treated as greenhouse
annual or short-lived
perennial.

Germination often seems to be most erratic, with good results one year and virtually nothing the next. To obtain consistent germination, sow coleus exactly as advised for busy lizzies but remove the clingfilm as soon as germination is well under way, otherwise damping-off, which is a fungus disease, may occur. It is a good idea to spray the seedlings every ten days with a thiram-based fungicide. Coleus, along with geraniums (page 105) and begonias (page 106) also benefit from a single spray with a systemic fungicide immediately after they are pricked out.

Pansies
Generally hardy
perennials treated as
half-hardy annuals.

Poor germination or total failure can be overcome by providing coolness but not cold – and darkness. Cover the seed very lightly and then cover the pot with black polythene or kitchen foil. Leave for a week and then check every other day. You should lift the covering for a

Pansies

very short moment in shade – anything more may slow germination down. Once germination is under way, remove the polythene or foil. The temperature throughout should not be more than 10°C (50°F).

Sweet peas
Hardy annual.

There are dangers in soaking sweet peas before sowing, as the seeds may die if they then encounter temporarily poor conditions, which may happen when sown in the open. Chipping is a good practice and especially effective with the darker-flowered sorts. However, rotting – whether in the open or under glass – is a prime cause of failure with sweet peas and treatment with a seed dressing can increase germination rates dramatically whether indoors or out.

12

ALPINES AND BULBS FROM SEED

*Or who needs specialists
anyway?*

Once upon a time, long long ago, there was a chap in the English Midlands who had an alpine plant nursery. It was rather well known for rare and difficult alpines but also carried a range of good plants for the ordinary rock garden. He propagated everything himself and did not buy any plants in.

Each year he would sow enough pots of seed to fill 12 large cold frames, which faced south in three ranks and were shaded with muslin. There were 15 of these frames in all, but three were usually occupied by pots of seed from the previous year that had not yet germinated. Now here is the interesting bit. He never once, in more than a decade, put any seed in the fridge. If seed needed to be sown in autumn, that's when it was sown, and he often split batches and sowed some seed when ripe and some the following spring. He also applied no artificial heat to any seeds. And who was he? Well, of course you have guessed and, yes, it was me.

DELAYED GERMINATION AND DORMANCY-BREAKING

So why am I telling you this, when I've already spent a lot of time discussing dormancy-breaking techniques? The answer is that I am doing so to reinforce the indication I gave you at the end of

Chapter 4 that dormancy can be said not really to exist at all and that dormancy-breaking methods merely hurry germination along to the convenience of the gardener. When I had my nursery system running, it did not matter if some seed took two or even three years to germinate as long as I could look after it properly meanwhile. Plenty of other things were coming along – so many, in fact, that I had more than time allowed me to deal with.

With so many perennials, alpines and bulbs, germination is delayed because of the patterns the plants have evolved which will allow them to germinate in assured environments where they can reach maturity. Fundamentally, if we leave them alone, they will germinate in due course. However, not everyone has 15 seed frames and if you have only one or two you will not want them cluttered up with dilatory seeds. For such gardeners, I have gone some long distance into research concerning methods of enhanced germination of perennials, alpines and bulbs, as well as woody plants. I must admit, too, that in the decades since I left the alpine trade, I have used the fridge and other methods just as avidly as anyone else and greatly enjoy the challenge of obtaining relatively quick results. The point is, though, that it is not *necessary* to do so – just convenient.

ALPINES AND THEIR SPECIAL TREATMENT

Alpines are for the most part perennials that have adapted to life in rocky, gravelly, extremely well-drained places, where harsh winds blow bearing sharp spicules of rock and snow lies as a surprisingly warm blanket for up to nine months of the year. You really do need different techniques if you are to be able to germinate alpines and grow them into mature plants.

CHOICE OF GROWING MEDIUM

First, do not use soil-less composts, as they are completely unsuitable for alpines. Instead, sow on a soil-based compost mixed with one third of its own volume of sharp grit. The very best grit you can get is sold by agricultural merchants as chick grit, and is made of flint. Its largest grade, which is turkey grit, makes the best possible top-dressing for alpine seed pots and for all alpines growing in pots.

CHOICE OF POT

I much prefer to use clay pots for alpines. The main reason for this is that, if the seeds do wait a long time before germinating, there is a much greater chance of plastic pots cracking, especially if you are tempted to pick them up one-handed. You should never do this with plastic pots, but everyone does. There is no doubt at all that plastic pots drain efficiently, but it is also perfectly true that alpines, from tiny seedlings to mature plants, thrive better in clays.

Small seeds should be lightly pressed into the soil, but a few might stick to the hands. Alpine seeds are often precious, so make sure to brush them off onto the compost. Alpines germinate best in clay pots. If you have only plastics, make the compost a little more gritty.

SOWING

Fill the pots with compost, level and firm them, but do not water at this stage. Now sow the seed on the surface, and, if it is large enough, press it gently into the surface. By the way, when you do this with any seeds, a few will stick to the palms of your hands or your fingers. You should always brush them back into the pot, making sure that they do not go anywhere else. Not doing this can be a major cause of strange seedlings cropping up where they should not, and it can lead to complete misidentification if the only seeds that germinate in a pot are stray ones from another batch. Then apply top-dressing.

WATERING

Hold the pot, whatever it is made of, in both hands and lower it into a bath of water. By 'bath' I mean anything that will hold water. You should not let the water level in the bath rise above the level of the top-dressing in the pot, but don't hold it too shallowly either, otherwise the compost will never become wet. When the top surface darkens, remove the pot and stand it to drain. If you have a suitable bath you can stand several pots in it at once and save a great deal of time.

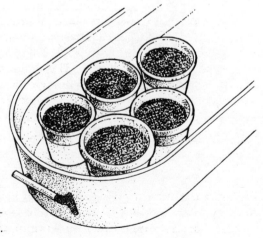

Placing clay pots of alpine seeds in a water bath. The bath must be relatively wide, otherwise the volume of water will not be enough to wet the compost up to the top. The water level should come to just below the compost surface and you should be able to top it up without sloshing it onto the compost.

This method should never be used for anything other than alpines. If you try it with a soil-less compost you will find that the top-layer floats off, taking seeds with it, and if you use it without a top-dressing it is likely that seeds will float away or at least be sufficiently disturbed to spoil your nice thin sowing.

Apart from that and using the fridge method that is cold stratification (pages 33–35) before sowing if you feel like speeding things up a bit, there is nothing more to sowing alpines, although to read some of the specialist amateur publications you would be forgiven for thinking it as complicated a business as cordon bleu cookery. The most elaborate recipes, with different composts in layers within the pot, ready to catch the roots at different stages of development, and with the most wonderfully specious quasi-scientific text to accompany the artwork, are as convincing to an experienced alpine sower as the propaganda of the age of Brezhnev. Gardening suffers, like so many other pastimes, from being the subject of over-elaboration by people who like to be seen to be doing something difficult. It isn't difficult. A little simple logic is all that's required.

BULBS

For bulbs, I use the same mixture that I have for alpines. This is because most bulbs like first-class drainage and also because a great many of them are alpines, inasmuch as they come from mountainous areas with gritty soils. Then, too, they need to be left in their pots for a longish time. This is not so much because they take a long time to germinate (although some do) but because they should not be moved for at least a year after germination and certainly not until a small bulb, corm or tuber has developed. Prick bulbs out too soon and you lose them.

SOWING BULB SEEDS

The great majority of bulb seeds should be sown as soon as ripe And, generally speaking, it is best to obtain bulb seeds from sources that can supply them in autumn at the latest. There are some exceptions, such as freesias and galtonias, which you can buy with confidence for winter or early spring delivery, but on the whole you should sow as soon as possible – which is often in summer – and simply place the pots in cold frames and wait. Tender bulbs, which include the freesias and galtonias I have mentioned, are better raised in the greenhouse.

You should always sow bulbs thinly so as to give them room to develop, and it is a good idea to give them just a little bonemeal during the growing season. Some bulbs, such as many of the lilies, grow very quickly and one or two will even flower in the same year as they are sown, but the great majority can be anything from three to five years before they reach the flowering stage and a few, such as *Cardiocrinum giganteum* may take seven.

Nevertheless, for many gardeners raising bulbs from seed is one of the most fascinating aspects of propagation. It really does test the patience, but the rewards are great. I remember (largely because it is in my records) sowing *Tulipa sprengeri* in 1971. It germinated in 1973 and I planted out the little bulbs in 1975. The first flowers appeared in 1977 and when I left that garden a year later (for such is life) there was the most beautiful drift of the mahogany-red blooms of this latest-flowering of all tulips.

13

VEGETABLES FROM SEED

*Or the nearest you will get to
something for nothing*

GOOD VEGETABLES NEED
GOOD SOIL

It is impossible to generalize about growing vegetables from seed, as each is so different from the next. You should, however, provide a well-worked soil that is as organic as possible. All this means is that it has been dug and as much well-rotted organic material added as you can find or afford. This can be stable or farmyard manure, garden compost, composted straw – anything. Just don't say that you can't get horse manure in a city. There is a convent in south London where the nuns grow the most wonderful vegetables fully organically and the local riding stables are only too glad to bring load after load of the stuff to their back gate. The better-run a stable is, the bigger its manure heap, and if you knew what an embarrassing land-grabber a manure heap is you would have not the least compunction about turning up with some plastic bags and offering to help reduce it.

I don't think that there can be any doubt that, in general, organically grown vegetables taste better, grow more consistently and crop better than others. There is no mystique about it and you do not have to wear special clothes or recite mantras or anything. Just use organic manures instead of artificial ones. If pests arrive, spray them. The thing is that you will find far fewer pests in an organic garden than in one that relies on artificials, and there tends to be a better biological balance.

SOWING AND PLANTING: A SELECTION

The sowing and planting dates I give below are only approximate and apply mainly to milder climates, so if you live in a colder area please allow for sowing a few weeks later. In more continental climates there is not the same danger of sudden late frosts or unusually mild early springs followed by frosts, but gardeners in such circumstances usually know perfectly well when gardening activities can start up for the year. It is as well to remember that a soil temperature below 5°C (41°C) causes plant growth to cease.

Many kinds of seed are sown into drills. These are simply scratches in the ground along which seeds are sown. You can use anything at all to make them. For hardy annuals, for example, I usually use an old pencil. For carrots I run a bit of thin stick along the garden line, while for larger seeds I walk backwards with the handle of the rake on the string and the corner of the blade marking out a v-shaped drill. Drills are made to the depth required for each kind of seed.

A double drill consists of two drills close together, the spaces between the double drills being the same as those advocated for single ones. Flat drills are taken out with the blade of a spade held almost parallel to the ground and are used mainly for peas and sometimes for beans.

An aubergine seedling in a peat pot.
It is at the stage when it is ready for
being planted, pot and all.

Artichoke, globe Sow in drills 30cm (1ft) apart and make sure you do so thinly and no more than 2.5cm (1in) deep. After germination, thin the seedlings to 25cm (10in) apart. Renew every four years. Mid-spring.

Asparagus Sow in drills 30cm (1ft) apart thinly and no more than 2.5cm (1in) deep. When the seedlings are about 7.5cm (3in) high, thin them out to 20cm (8in) apart. The following year, transplant into specially prepared beds Mid-spring.

Aubergine Sow in individual pots under glass with the temperature at about 20°C (68°F). Peat pots are a good idea, as you can then plant the entire pot in a greenhouse bed or out of doors in milder areas. Harden them off before planting outside. Sow indoor crop in late winter, outdoors in early spring.

Broad beans Sow 5cm (2in) deep in double drills 60cm (2ft) apart or in flat ones (taken out with the flat of the spade) at the same distance, in which the seeds are in a double row. Sow in early spring or mid-spring or under cloches in late winter.

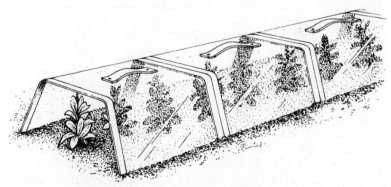

Young bean plants under cloches in the open ground.

French beans	Sow in single drills 5cm (2in) deep. The drills should be 45cm (18in) apart and the seed should be sown 5cm (2in) deep. Late spring.
Runner beans	Sow 5cm (2in) deep. They should be no closer than 25cm (10in) apart. Sow when the danger of frosts is over.
Beets for leaves Swiss chard, ruby chard	Sow 10–15cm (4–6in) apart in drills 45cm (18in) apart. The fruits, each of which contains several seeds, few of which germinate, should be no more than 2.5cm (1in) deep. Mid-spring.
Beetroot	Sow as for leaf beets but with the drills 30cm (1ft) apart and with two fruits at each station. Germination is improved by soaking for 24 hours beforehand and it is a good idea to net the young seedlings against birds. Mid-spring.
Broccoli	Sow thinly 1cm (about $^1/_2$in) deep in drills 15cm (6in) apart in a seedbed. Thin to 10cm (4in). Transplant to where they are to grow at 45cm (18in) apart when they are 7.5cm (3in) high. Mid-spring to late spring.
Brussels sprouts	Sow in the seedbed as for broccoli and transplant at about 10cm (4in) high. They should be put 75cm (30in) apart. Early to mid-spring.
Cabbage	Sow in the seedbed as for broccoli but choose varieties for succession and sow some every so often. Spring cabbage in mid-summer and late summer, summer cabbages in mid-spring, winter cabbages, savoys and red cabbage in mid-spring and late spring. Chinese cabbage, which is becoming very popular, is best sown in mid-summer and late summer for cropping in mid-autumn. Transplant on average 45cm (18in) apart when the plants look sturdy and have a cluster of leaves.

Capsicum

Sow under glass at about 20°C (68°F) in peat pots. Sow two seeds to a pot and keep the stronger one. For greenhouse cultivation sow in late winter, for outside sow in early spring. They are much better grown under glass, however.

Carrots

Sow *very* thinly in shallow drills 15cm (6in) apart. The more thinly you sow, the less you have to thin the seedlings, and it is the act of thinning that creates the carroty odour that attracts the carrot fly. Sow successionally from mid-spring to early summer.

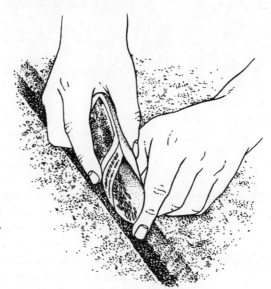

Very thin sowing of carrots means less thinning of young plants and thus less trouble from carrot fly. Draw a shallow drill to hold the very small seeds.

Cauliflower

Sow very thinly in the seed bed as for cabbages. Transplant when they have about half a dozen leaves, setting the plants at about 75cm (30in) centres. Sow autumn cauliflowers from mid-spring to late spring, winter ones in late spring, and summer varieties in early mid-spring.

Setting plants at x unit centres

It's much more accurate to speak of setting plants at x unit centres rather than at x units apart. It simply means that the centres of the plants are that distance apart and is a somewhat jargonistic but universal term used by the more logical professional gardeners. Consider heather plants advocated to be planted 45cm (18in) apart Buy some super specimens 30 cm (1ft) across and the centreswill be almost a metre (3ft) apart. Purchase rooted cuttings and the centres will be 45cm (18in) apart - half as much. But advocate 'at 45cm (18in) centres' and 30cm (1ft) specimens will be about 23cm (9in) apart but they and the rooted cuttings will be at the same true distance from one another. The difference is in fact crucial and the 'centres' formula eliminates the variable introduced by the varying diameters of plants at different stages of growth.

Celeriac   Sow under glass in early spring, putting two seeds in each peat pot and eventually removing the weaker seedling. Harden off and plant in late spring.

Celery   Sow under glass in early spring at about 13°C (55°F) in peat pots. Try to maintain this amount of warmth after germination, as a drop in temperature for more than 12 hours can cause the plants to bolt when they are mature. Harden off carefully before planting, which should be done when the plants are large enough to handle. Do not cover celery seeds, as they need light for germination.

Chicory   Sow very thinly in shallow drills 30 cm (1ft) apart in late spring or early summer. Germination rates are very high, so thin sowing is vital. Thin the seedlings to 15cm (6in) apart.

Cucumber, greenhouse	Set each seed sideways in the compost in a peat pot so that there is about 1cm (¹/₂in) of compost above it. Germinate under glass with a highish temperature (21–26°C/70–80°F). Early spring.
Cucumber, outdoor or ridge	Sow in *gentle* heat in mid-spring and plant out after the frost danger has gone in late spring, or sow towards the end of late spring out of doors, setting the seeds 2.5cm (1in) deep and in pairs, thinning to one seedling after germination. Cover with cloches.
Endive	Sow directly in shallow drills 30cm (1ft) apart for curly types (which should be sown from mid-spring to late summer) or 38cm (15in) apart for broad-leaved endives (which you should sow from mid-summer to early autumn). Thin in the rows to these distances and transplant the thinnings. This will help to give successional cropping.
Kohl rabi	Sow very thinly in shallow drills 30cm (1ft) apart and thin the seedlings to 25cm (10in). Sow successionally from late winter to early summer if you are using green forms, and from early summer to early autumn for purple ones.

Leeks

Always use a dibber in the open ground, and never your finger as you would when transplanting seedlings in pots. Fill the planting holes for leeks with water, not soil.

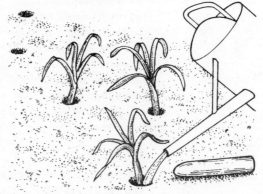

Leeks	Sow very thinly in the seed bed in shallow drills 15cm (6in) apart and transplant when they are about 20cm (8in) high, which is usually in early summer. Make holes with a dibber and puddle the transplants in with water, allowing the water to wash the soil into the holes – don't fill them with soil by hand.

Lettuce
Cabbage lettuce;
Cos lettuce;
loose-leaf lettuce

Lettuce are divided into
(1) Cabbage lettuce, subdivided into
(a) Butterheads, which have soft leaves
(b) Crispheads, which have crisp leaves
(2) Cos lettuce
(3) Salad Bowl or loose-leaf lettuce, which are non-hearting and from which you can cut individual leaves over a period.
● Different varieties among the groups provide crops at different times of year and sowings can be made as follows:
● For crops in summer and autumn – the main crop of lettuce – sow outdoors in mid-spring to early summer.
● For cropping in early winter, sow in late summer.
● For lettuce in mid-winter sow under glass in early autumn or mid-autumn.
● For spring lettuce sow winter-hardy varieties outdoors in late summer or early autumn for late spring cropping, or sow in mid-autumn under cloches for a slighty earlier crop.
High temperatures inhibit germination of lettuces and they do not transplant well either in summer temperatures. Therefore the greatest activity in lettuce-raising is either side of the hot weather, but this will vary greatly according to the climate of the part of the country in which you live.

Leaf lettuce

Leaf lettuce is a crop obtained by sowing Cos varieties close together to encourage leaves

---

Leaf lettuce

rather than hearts. You then cut the leaves 2.5cm (1in) above the soil and leave the stump to produce a second crop about six weeks later. Sow in rows 12cm (5in) apart and so that the plants are only 2.5cm (1in) apart in the rows. If you sow one square metre (or one square yard) per week from mid-spring to late spring, this will give you enough lettuce for the average family from late spring to mid-summer, with the second cut providing a crop from early mid-summer to late summer. Weekly sowings thereafter in late summer will provide lettuce leaves from the end of late summer to mid-autumn. Remember to use Cos-varieties.

Gourds
Marrows, courgettes, pumpkins and squashes

Sowing can be done outside or under glass, but you should be aware that none of these will germinate if the soil temperature is below 13°C (55°F). Out of doors, sow three seeds at each site, which should be between 90 and 120cm (3–4ft) apart, no earlier than late spring. After germination select the strongest seedling at each station. It is best to cover each seed site with a cloche or glass jar. Under glass, sow a month earlier in soil blocks or peat pots. Harden off very carefully and plant out four to five weeks after sowing.

Onions
Bulb onions

You should take good care to make a seedbed-type soil for onions, with a fine tilth and well firmed. Onions from seed are a poor proposition in cold, wet soils and are best sown in soil that has been covered with cloches or clear polythene for a while to encourage it to warm up. Sow very thinly from early spring to mid-spring in shallow drills 30cm (1ft) apart. Thinning to 5cm (2in) will give a good crop of medium onions, and further thinning to 10cm (4in) will allow you to grow large ones. You can use the thinnings for salads.

Pickling onions   Sow thinly in early or mid-spring in drills 23cm (9in) wide – the width of the blade of a spade. Do not thin: they will sort themselves out.

Spring onions   Sow successively from early spring to early summer about every 2 weeks in rows 10cm (4in) apart. Be sure to sow thinly so that you do not have to do any thinning before pulling.

Shallots   Although usually grown from sets, shallots are excellent from seed of F1 hybrids such as 'Creation', which can be sown in early and mid-spring for cropping about a month later than those raised from sets. The thinnings can be used for salads.

Parsley   The germination of parsley can be slow, and indeed practically non-existent if sown in cold or wet weather. Always sow when the soil is warm. You can water the drills with boiling water just before sowing. During the

Preparing the drill for parsley.

Parsley	germination period, which can be up to six weeks, keep the soil moist but use tepid water. The drills should be about 1cm (¹/₂in) deep and the plants should eventually be 15cm(6in) apart.

Parsnip

Parsnip seed is not very easy, as it loses its viability quickly and must be fresh, and germinates very poorly in cold conditions. Although you may find early spring or even late winter sowings recommended, it is much better to leave them until mid- or late spring or sow under glass in gentle heat in soil blocks or peat pots. Sow three seeds at each station with the stations 15cm (6in) apart and do so on a calm day, as the seed is light and can blow away.

Peas

In general, wrinkle peas are sweeter than round peas, but round ones are hardier and best used for very early and very late sowings. Sow in flat drills 23cm (9in) wide (the width of the blade of a spade), setting them at 10cm (4in) intervals in interlocking fives at a depth of 5cm (2in). Sow in early spring for a midsummer crop. The varieties should be round-seeded or first early wrinkled. A sowing of a second early wrinkled variety a few weeks later will produce a crop in mid-summer.

Alternatively, early and second early peas (for example. 'Kelvedon Wonder') can be sown successively at intervals of three weeks from mid-spring to early summer. 'Kelvedon Wonder' can also be sown in early and mid-summer for an autumn crop.

Mangetouts

Mangetout peas are best sown in mid-spring or early spring but successional sowings from early spring to early summer can spread the cropping period of these increasingly popular peas.

Petit pois

You can sow a petit pois (dwarf) variety in mid-summer for cropping in autumn, but this works reliably only in the drier, sunnier areas.

Radishes

It is pointless to get technical about radishes – just sow them shallowly and *thinly* and wait for the results. It is best to make small sowings at frequent intervals. One way to speed up their germination is to take out a shallow drill, water it, and then cover the seed with dry soil.

Spinach
Perpetual spinach

This is spinach beet and should be sown as other leaf beets (see page 118).

New Zealand spinach

Sow New Zealand spinach in drills 30cm (1ft) apart with three seeds to each 60cm (2ft) station, reducing to one after germination. Sow 2.5cm (1in) deep. Mid- and late spring.

Spinach

True spinach is sown thinly 2.5cm (1in) deep in drills 30cm (1ft) apart, thinning the seedlings to 7.5cm (3in) intervals. Mid- and late spring.

Sweet corn

Start off under glass in individual peat pots, harden off, and plant out at 45cm (18in) intervals. Sow in rectangular blocks, not in a single row, in order to assist wind pollination.

Tomatoes
Greenhouse varieties

Sow two seeds in each individual peat pot in mid-winter if the greenhouse is heated or early spring if it is not. The latter is much more economical and the plants should be planted in late spring. The seed should be germinated in gentle heat, as it will not do so if the temperature is below 10°C (50°F). Reduce to one seedling per pot after germination.

Outdoor varieties

The procedure is the same as for the unheated greenhouse but sow later – in mid-spring – for planting out in late spring or early summer.

Tomatoes   Great advances are being made in the breeding of tomatoes. Always read the catalogue carefully for indications of types that will suit your needs and especially for flavour. The packets usually carry full instructions.

14

SOME LESS EASY TREES AND SHRUBS

Abies species
SILVER FIRS
Evergreen coniferous trees

Germination rate is low because of a high proportion of unformed seed. Most species benefit from cold treatment in moist peat for 28 days at 1.5°C (35°F) but small quantities of seed may be sown untreated in early spring after the embryos have been dissected out (i.e. surgically removed from the seed coats).

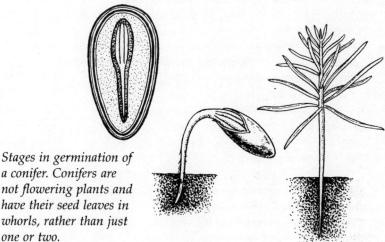

Stages in germination of a conifer. Conifers are not flowering plants and have their seed leaves in whorls, rather than just one or two.

Abutilon vitifolium
Evergreen large shrub or small tree

Sow in early spring with bottom heat.

***Acacia* species** WATTLES Evergreen, small trees	Pour boiling water onto the seeds and allow to soak for 24 hours, then sow immediately. Gently free the seed leaves from the seed coats if necessary when seedlings are growing. *Acacia dealbata* is the 'mimosa' of florists.
***Acer* species** MAPLES Deciduous shrubs or small trees	The viability of most maples is low and they are vulnerable to drying. Sow in autumn, except for spring-ripened seed, which should be sown on collection. *Acer griseum* is very difficult but some success has been obtained by sowing dissected-out embryos.
***Aesculus* species** HORSE CHESTNUTS; BUCKEYES Deciduous, shrubby or tall trees	Vulnerable to drying. Sow on collection; germination will occur in spring. The seed leaves (cotyledons) do not appear above the soil.
Ailanthus altissima TREE OF HEAVEN Deciduous, tall tree	Give cold treatment for two months in moist peat at 1.5°C (35°F) or a little higher.
Albizia julibrissin SILK TREE Deciduous small tree	Treat as for *Acacia* or chip the seed coats.
***Alnus* species** ALDERS Deciduous medium trees	Sow in early spring.
***Aloysia triphylla* (syn. *Lippia citriodora*)** LEMON-SCENTED VERBENA Deciduous, medium-sized aromatic shrub	Genetically, a proportion (approximately 25 per cent) of the seeds are unfilled and cannot germinate.

Amelanchier
lamarckii
SNOWY MESPILUS
Deciduous small tree

Differential dormancy allows small germination of spring-sown seed. Cold treatment by sowing in pots in unheatedframe in autumn will give better results.

Aralia species
ANGELICA TREES
Deciduous small trees

Low germination rate due to proportion of unfilled seed. Cold treatment for 30 days at to 1.5°C (35°F) followed by warming and further chilling for three weeks.

Arbutus species
STRAWBERRY TREES
Evergreen large
shrubs

Soak fruits in water to soften them and then remove the seeds from the pulp and dry. Drying the fruit is difficult as moulds often intrude. Sow immediately in an unheated frame or in spring after cold treatment for one month at 1.5°C (35°F).

The rather messy business of separating arbutus seeds from their pulp is preferable to the risk of losing them to moulds if you try to dry the fruits first.

Aronia species
CHOKEBERRIES
Small deciduous
shrubs

Remove seed from fruits, whether fresh from the garden or dried from the seed company. Cold treatment for two months at 1.5°C (35°F) gives adequate germination. Alternating cold and warm is the optimum treatment but is not necessary for amateur requirements.

***Athrotaxis* species** TASMANIAN CEDAR Slow-growing conifer	Sow as soon as obtained and place the pots in a cool place out of doors. Germination may be long delayed.

Azalea* see *Rhododendron

Azara serrata Medium evergreen shrub	Extract seed from the white berries (formed in hot summers) and sow with bottom heat in early spring.
***Berberis* species** BARBERRIES Small or medium evergreen or deciduous shrubs	Berberis are easy from seed if sown in autumn. Either whole berries or individual seeds may be sown. Spring-sown seed gives much-reduced germination.
***Betula* species** BIRCHES Deciduous medium trees	Sow in early spring. If the frame is in sun use very light shading. Do not cover the seed. Light is necessary for germination.
Broussonetia ***papyrifera*** PAPER MULBERRY Deciduous large shrub or small tree	When seed can be obtained, sow in early spring with bottom heat. Plant out at least three to obtain berries.
***Buddleja* species** Mostly deciduous shrubs	Easy from spring-sown seed. *B davidii* can become a weed: best to buy named varieties. *B. colvilei* has large, deep rose flowers and is eminently desirable. It germinates abundantly but is slightly tender.
Callicarpa bodinieri **var. *giraldii*** Smallish shrub	Germination varies from year to year. Sometimes adequate from an early spring sowing, sometimes a failure. Cold treatment of extracted berries in moist peat can give good results but can also fail. It is said to need several specimens to ensure the production of berries but this is not necessarily so.

Callistemon species
BOTTLEBRUSHES
Evergreen shrubs,
small but medium in
warm climates

Very easy from spring-sown seed with bottom heat but treat against damping-off disease.

Carpenteria
californica
TREE ANEMONE
Evergreen medium
shrub

Very easy from spring-sown seed, but seedlings are almost always inferior to clonally propagated specimens.

Carpinus species
HORNBEAMS
Deciduous medium
trees

Harvest the seed while it is still slightly green and sow immediately in a cold frame. Germination the following spring.

Carya species
HICKORIES
Deciduous medium
trees

Outside the USA imported American nuts must be used. Cold treatment, either in moist peat or on their own in a plastic bag for two months at 1.5°C (35°F). If nuts are received direct from cold storage, sow at once.

Ceanothus species
CALIFORNIAN LILACS
Small to medium or
large shrubs, ever-
green or deciduous

Seed is not readily set outside the USA but is quite often offered for sale in Europe. Germination is quite good if the seeds are soaked in boiling water and left in the cooling water for 24 hours.

Cedrus species
CEDARS
Large evergreen
coniferous trees

Germination is easy in spring. Cones may be stored unopened until then, when they will open in hot water. Storage of naked seed is unwise, as they are oily and soon deteriorate. *C. brevifolia* is a slow-growing small tree

---

Chamaecyparis
species
FALSE CYPRESSES
Evergreen conifers,
medium to large

Poor germination rates because of unfilled seed. Cones open and release seeds if dried in the sun. Differing dormancies between batches mean that seedlings sometimes appear in batches or a few at a time in successive years.

Chamaerops *humilis* DWARF FAN PALM, EUROPEAN PALM Small evergreen	Sowing in spring with bottom heat gives small germination. Warm treatment – in moist peat at 70–75°C (21–24°F) – produces an improvement, but seeds may germinate during the treatment and there should in any case be signs of germination after 14 days.
Chimonanthus *praecox* WINTERSWEET Deciduous medium shrub	Seed is occasionally offered and should be sown as soon as obtained.
Colletia species Evergreen medium shrubs, foliage mainly spines	Occasionally sets abundant seed, which must be caught as soon as it drops, as the plants are too spiny to handle. It germinates prolifically if sown in bottom heat in early spring.
Cordyline australis NEW ZEALAND CABBAGE PALM Evergreen small tree	Not to be confused with the cabbage palm, *Sabal palmetto*, which is the state tree of Florida. This is a member of the lily family and not a true palm at all. Seeds germinate well in spring but need bottom heat.
Cotoneaster species Evergreen or deciduous, prostrate shrubs to small trees	Such a common genus should be easy from seed but is not. Many are doubly dormant because of hard seed coats and internal (embryo) dormancy. Seed, removed from the berries, may be rubbed between sheets of sandpaper (see page 37) to scarify the seed coats and then given alternating warm and cold treatment in moist peat.
Crataegus species THORNS; HAWTHORNS Medium shrubs and small trees	Germination is difficult. Sow immediately when ripe, having extracted the seed from the berries. Place the pots in a frame but early enough for thorough warming to take place. Subsequently, allow a winter's chilling. Seedlings should appear in mid-spring but some species may take a further year.

Cupressus species
CYPRESSES
Medium to large,
evergreen conifers

Treat seed with a fungicide powder and give cold treatment for one month at 1.5°C (35°F).

Cytisus species
BROOMS
Small to medium
shrubs

Soak seeds of all species in boiling water and allow to cool for 24 hours. *C. battandieri*, the pineapple broom, does not need this and germinates well with bottom heat in spring.

Daphne species
Mainly small shrubs

Remove seed from the berries while they are slightly unripe and sow immediately. This is usually in mid-summer. Alternatively give cold treatment in moist peat for three months at 1.5°C (35°F). Seed should not be dry-stored, as it will lose its viability and germination will be poor. Net the berries of *D. mezereum*, which are poisonous to mammals, against birds.

**Davidia
involucrata**
HANDKERCHIEF TREE;
GHOST TREE; DOVE
TREE
Deciduous small to
medium tree

The fruit has a dry flesh, within which is a ribbed nut containing three to five seeds. Many failures occur when the nut is sown whole. It should be split and the seeds extracted and sown immediately.

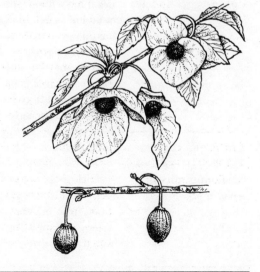

*The incredibly hard
nuts of* Davidia
involucrata *should be
split open to extract
the seeds. If you sow
the whole nut, you
may have to wait many
years for germination.*

Dipelta floribunda
Medium shrub

It is sometimes recommended that seed should be sown in an outdoor seed bed. I tried everything with home-saved seed for ten years and eventually gave up, having raised not a single seedling. The seeds appear filled but the embryos are under-developed.

Embothrium coccineum
CHILEAN FIRE BUSH
Small semi-evergreen to evergreen tree or large shrub

Seed germinates well with bottom heat in spring in a lime-free compost but the seedlings sometimes refuse to grow on and are probably sensitive to dryness. It is debatable whether it is worth sowing, as named forms are so superior.

Enkianthus campanulatus
Deciduous, small to medium shrub

A lime-hater, so use an ericaceous compost. Sow in early spring and do not cover the seeds.

Eucalyptus species
GUMS
Evergreen small shrubs to large trees

Sow with bottom heat on the surface of the compost in early spring. Do not cover except for the larger seeds of tropical species. Seeds are black among red-orange unfertilized ovules. Contrary to the advice of many authorities, I have found that adequate germination is obtained *without exception* in over 70 species, including several for which the need for special treatment has been claimed.

Eucryphia lucida
Evergreen medium shrub

Eucryphia lucida is the only eucryphia with whose seed I have had first-hand experience. It was sown in early spring in a lime-free compost with bottom heat and it germinated quite well.

Euonymus species
Small, medium and large evergreen shrubs

Seed stores badly and becomes profoundly dormant if sowing is delayed so is best sown when fresh in autumn. This will also break dormancy and produce a good germination the following spring.

Fagus **species**
BEECHES
Deciduous large trees

Beech nuts (mast) should be sown immediately in a cold frame: they will not tolerate becoming dry. Imported seed arriving late should be cold-treated for one month at 1.5°C (35°F).

Fatsia japonica
Medium evergreen shrub

Remove the seed from the fruits and sow with bottom heat in spring. Fair germination.

Fraxinus **species**
ASHES
Deciduous tall trees

It is essential to sow immediately upon collection. Sow in individual pots in a cold frame. Germination may take place over two or three years.

Fremontodendron californicum
Evergreen scandent shrub

Easy from seed but the seedlings will be inferior to the hybrid 'California Glory' and therefore sowing is not recommended.

Gaultheria **species**
Evergreen dwarf to small shrubs

Lime-haters, so should be sown in ericaceous compost. Cold treatment is desirable but in general adequate germination will result from spring sowing.

Genista **species**
BROOMS
Small to medium shrubs, some small trees

Despite belonging to the pea family, most of which have hard seed coats, genistas mostly germinate quite well from untreated, spring-sown seed. Bottom heat is an advantage. The Mount Etna broom, *Genista aetnensis*, germinates freely in this way.

Ginkgo biloba
MAIDENHAIR TREE
Tall tree

Seed is not set by female trees until they are well past 50 years old and is encased in a fruit that smells just like dog droppings. It is not worth trying to germinate it. Imported seed, however, should be soaked in boiling water in spring and allowed to cool for 24 hours, prior to sowing with bottom heat. *Ginkgo* seeds have immature embryos that mature after the fruit have fallen.

Gleditsia species LOCUSTS Small trees	Boiling water treatment in spring.
Grevillea species Small shrubs	Good seeds are seldom set in cultivation, but imported seed should be sown with bottom heat or in a propagating case at 15.5°C (60°F). Soak in water for 24 hours first.
Gymnocladus dioica KENTUCKY COFFEE TREE Deciduous slow-growing tree	Soak seeds in boiling water and allow to cool for 24 hours before sowing in spring.
Hippophaë rhamnoïdes SEA BUCKTHORN Deciduous medium shrub	Remove seeds from berries. Give cold treatment for three months at 1.5°C (35°F) or a little higher, then sow in spring.
Ilex species HOLLIES Evergreen shrubs or trees	Dormancy in hollies is very profound and compounded by hard seed coats. Extract seed from the berries and sow in individual pots in a cold frame. Forget all about them and allow yourself to be surprised when seedlings appear a few at a time over three years or even more time.
Juniperus species JUNIPERS Evergreen conifers of various sizes	Junipers are very difficult to germinate. The best thing to do is to remove the seeds from the berries, sow them, put them in a cold frame and trust to luck. You may be rewarded with odd seedlings appearing from time to time.
Koelreuteria paniculata GOLDEN RAIN TREE Deciduous small tree	Spring-sown, untreated seed will germinate but very poorly. Scarification by rubbing between sheets of sandpaper increases germination dramatically.

Kolkwitzia
amabilis
BEAUTY BUSH
Deciduous small to
medium shrub

Some germination results from untreated
spring sowing with bottom heat. Cold
treatment for 30 days at 1.5°C (35°F) appears to
give better results.

Laburnum **species**
Deciduous medium
shrubs

The seeds are poisonous, as is the rest of the
plant. Germination is good if the seed is
scarified between sheets of sandpaper (see
page 37) or if it is individually chipped (see
page 36).

Laurus nobilis
CULINARY BAY
Medium to large
evergreen shrub

Remove flesh from seeds and sow in autumn if
possible. Otherwise soak in warm water (not
boiling) and allow to stand for 24 hours before
sowing.

Leycesteria
formosa
Deciduous medium
shrub

Extract the seed from the berries and sow in
spring.

Lippia citriodora see *Aloysia triphylla*

Liriodendron
tulipifera
TULIP TREE
Large deciduous tree

Ideally, sow in autumn. Spring-sown seed
should be given cold treatment for about six
weeks at 1.5°C (35°F).

Lonicera **species**
HONEYSUCKLES
Deciduous or ever-
green, small to
medium shrubs or
vigorous climbers.

Spring-sown seed gives adequate germination
in some species, others need cold treatment,
while still others may require alternating warm
and cold. Probably the best idea is to sow all of
them when available and then expect delayed
germination, a few at a time.

Maclura pomifera
OSAGE ORANGE
Deciduous large
shrub or small tree

Spring sowings: soak in water for 24 hours.

Magnolia **species**
Evergreen or
deciduous medium
shrubs to large trees

Seeds are enclosed in a bright orange or red
pulp. Lay them out to dry in the sun and the
seeds will be freed from the pulp. Sow immediately in individual pots in a cold frame. Bought
seed, arriving late, may be given cold treatment
for 30 days at 1.5°C (35°F) but storage can
reduce the viability of the oily seeds.

Malus **species**
CRAB APPLES
Deciduous small trees

Spring germination is very difficult. Crab
apples should be sown in the autumn in
individual pots in a cold frame. Do not attempt
to propagate named cultivars by seed, as the
seedlings will be inferior. Whip-and-tongue
grafting in spring is best left to professionals.

Menziesia **species**
Small lime-hating
shrubs

Sow in spring on the surface of an ericaceous
compost and do not cover the seed.

Myrtus **species**
MYRTLES
Small to large shrubs

Extract seeds from fresh or dried berries and
sow in spring with bottom heat.

Nothofagus **species**
SOUTHERN BEECHES
Small to large ever-
green or deciduous
trees, often beech-like

Sow individually in pots in a cold frame in
autumn.

Olearia **species**
NEW ZEALAND DAISY
BUSHES
Evergreen, wind-
resistant shrubs

Sow in spring with bottom heat. Failure is
usually due to unfilled seed set in cultivation.

Oxydendrum
arboreum
SORREL TREE
Large shrub or small
tree. Lime-hater.

Treat as for *Rhododendron*.

***Paeonia* species** TREE PEONIES Medium to fairly large shrubs	Double dormancy. Sowing in spring (a period of chilling is not always necessary) results in the production of the root. A subsequent period of cold, followed by warm, will induce shoot production. Either leave for a year or give a (second) period of cold artificially. Protect from mice.
Paulownia ***tomentosa*** FOXGLOVE TREE Deciduous medium tree	Germination is very easy, but seedlings are extremely prone to damping-off and sowing should be thin. Do not cover the seed: light is essential.
***Penstemon* species** Dwarf shrubs	Sow in late winter in a cold frame. Germination is best in cool conditions, i.e. no more than 15°C (60°F) by day and 10°C (50°F) by night, but is not usually more than about 50 per cent. This is adequate, of course.
Phellodendron ***amurense*** AMUR CORK TREE Deciduous medium tree	Stored seed must be kept cool. Imported seed is often not of good quality but the few seedlings that result are enough for gardeners.
***Phormium* species** NEW ZEALAND FLAX Technically evergreen perennials	I have had no success whatever with home-saved seed, which is set in abundance but is almost all unfilled. Imported seed from New Zealand should germinate well as long as it is not too old.
***Phyllodoce* species** Evergreen dwarf shrubs of the heather family	Treat as for *Rhododendron*.
***Pieris* species** Evergreen small to medium shrubs	Treat as for *Rhododendron*.

Picea species
SPRUCES
Evergreen medium to
large conifers

Sow in spring in a cold frame (unheated).
Germination is good if the seed has been
stored well.

Pinus species
PINES
Small to very large
evergreen conifers

Sow in late autumn or early winter for
germination the following spring. Place in a
cold frame without bottom heat. It is important
not to sow too early in autumn, as pine
seedlings do not take kindly to frost. Sown in
spring, dormancy will have built up and cold
treatment will become necessary.

**_Piptanthus_
laburnifolius**
EVERGREEN
LABURNUM
Large shrub, partly
evergreen

Rubbing between sheets of sandpaper or
chipping the seed coats assists germination, but
results are surprisingly good with no treatment
at all.

**_Pittosporum_
species**
Evergreen medium to
large shrubs

Sow the sticky seeds as soon as they are ripe.
Place in heat in early spring.

Populus species
POPLARS
Deciduous trees,
mostly large

Poplars are difficult. The difficulty is not in
initiating germination; that is quite easy as long
as the seeds are not covered – they require
light. It is the absolute necessity of maintaining
an even degree of moisture that is beyond most
amateurs, who usually cannot keep a constant
watch. Over-wetting is fatal, but so is any
degree of drying, especially at the stage when
the seed coat has been raised above the
compost but has not yet been shed.

Protea species
Small to medium
evergreen shrubs

There is a growing interest in trying these magnificent South African shrubs out of doors in
mild gardens and in conservatories elsewhere.
Germination is difficult, but _P. cynaroïdes_ and _P._

Protea species

barbigera have proved relatively easy when sown in spring in heat at around 21°C (70°F) and with high humidity. This regime will suit most of them but germination rates are low and seeds expensive.

Prunus species
A large genus, from small shrubs to medium trees

Prunus seeds have stony coats which, surprisingly, are not a barrier to germination. Almonds germinate better when the stone is cracked open but in general it is embryo dormancy that has to be overcome. This can be done by cold treatment in damp peat at 2–4°C (36–40°F) but I suggest you should sow in an unheated frame in autumn.

Pyracantha species
FIRETHORNS
Evergreen medium shrubs

The method is to remove the seeds from the berries and sow immediately in an unheated frame. However, the disease fireblight is now so prevalent that I cannot recommend growing pyracanthas from seed and must suggest that you buy a named variety with a known resistance to the disease.

Quercus species
OAKS
Medium shrubs to mighty trees

Acorns exemplify seeds with high moisture contents which must be sown immediately after ripening.

Quercus species

Oaks are divided into the white oaks (e.g. *Quercus robur, Q. bicolor*) and the black oaks (such as *Q. rubra* and *Q. coccinea*). Such vernacular names as red oak and scarlet oak have nothing to do with the black and white divisions. All acorns should be sown as soon as they are collected, although despatch by air will be quick enough if they are sown as soon as they arrive.

White oaks will begin to germinate right away, but black oaks will wait until the following spring, as they have embryo dormancy which is absent in the white oaks. Black oaks will dry out fatally if sowing is delayed until spring, so there is no point in trying treatments used for other seeds with embryo dormancy. As long as you sow in autumn it is not necessary to know which oaks are white and which are black.

Rhododendron **species**
Dwarf to large shrubs; some trees. The majority are evergreen but some (including many azaleas) are deciduous. Lime-haters.

Rhododendrons should be sown in spring in a place where they will not be subject to frost. A temperature of 7°C (45°F) is ideal and this can be provided in a frost-free greenhouse. Cold-frame sowings should be delayed until all but light ground frosts are over. Rhododendrons are therefore best sown after most other trees and shrubs. Sow in the surface of a soil-less, lime-free (ericaceous) compost and allow plenty of light but no direct sunshine. Do *not* sow in autumn, as the seedlings are too small to survive without constant attention. Prick out when large enough to handle without injury either to the upper parts of the plants or the tiny root systems.

Rhus **species**
Sumachs
Deciduous large shrubs

In spring soak seed in very hot water and allow to continue to soak for 24 hours before sowing.

Robinia species
FALSE ACACIAS
Deciduous small to
medium trees

Soak in boiling water and allow to cool for
24 hours before a spring sowing.

Rosa species
Small to medium
shrubs, climbers

Roses germinate best when the seeds are
extracted from the hips as soon as they have
turned red. Further delay may cause drying,
which will delay or reduce germination.
Dormancy is caused by the seed coats and
autumn sowing is preferable so as to allow
substances in the seed coats to leach away
naturally. Pots or trays may be brought into
heat with advantage in spring.

Rosmarinus
ROSEMARY
Small aromatic
evergreen shrubs

Seed may be as much as 55 per cent unfilled.

Rubus species
ORNAMENTAL
BRAMBLES
Deciduous, semi-ever-
green or evergreen
shrubs and woody-
stemmed, scrambling
climbers

Put the berries in water in a food blender to
separate the seeds from the pulp and sow in
autumn in an unheated frame. Germination
may be delayed by from one to three years
from the following spring

Salix species
WILLOWS
Small to medium
deciduous trees

Willow seed is extremely vulnerable to
becoming even slightly dry. It should be collected as soon as the capsules start to turn yellow and should be sown without delay.
Germination is extremely rapid and may occur
in as little as one or two days.

Sambucus species
ELDERS
Deciduous medium
shrubs or trees

Elders have hard seed coats and embryo
dormancy. They may be sown in autumn but
germination may be delayed for 18 months or
more. Alternatively, the seed can be soaked in

Sambucus species	water for 24 hours in mid-winter and then given cold treatment for three months at 1.5°C (35°F) in sand or vermiculite.
Sorbus species MOUNTAIN ASHES; WHITEBEAMS Small to medium trees	The best results are obtained from sowing as soon as the seeds can be removed from the ripe berries. Spring sowings should follow ten weeks of cold treatment at temperatures only just above freezing, using moist sand or peat. Without treatment, spring sowings may wait one or two years before germinating.
Symphoricarpos **species** SNOWBERRY Deciduous small shrubs	Too difficult. Not worth it.
Styrax species SNOWBELLS Deciduous small trees	Difficult but worth every effort. Soak in water for three days and then give cold treatment at 1.5°C (35°F) for six weeks. Alternatively, sow in an unheated frame in autumn.
Telopea truncata TASMANIAN WARATAH Deciduous small to medium shrub	Beware of unfilled seed. Good seed, if it can be obtained, germinates quite well in spring with bottom heat.
Taxus species YEWS Evergreen conifers; shrubs or small trees	Very slow germination. Although varying degrees of cold treatment work quite well there is little gain over autumn sowing, as seedlings may not appear for a year or two anyway. Complicated systems of warming and chilling are sometimes used.
Trachycarpus fortunei CHUSAN PALM Evergreen palm	Sow in spring at 24°C (75°F).

Vaccinium species
BILBERRIES,
BLUEBERRIES,
CRANBERRIES ETC.
Evergreen small, lime-
hating shrubs

Once the berries have become very dark and show a bloom on the surface, remove the seeds and dry well before storing. Sow on the surface of an ericaceous compost in an unheated frame in spring. Germination may be very rapid over part of the sowing and then further seedlings may emerge over the next two years.

Viburnum species
Small to medium
evergreen or
deciduous shrubs

This is a very large genus, so it is not possible to give hard and fast guidance. Most, however, exhibit double dormancy, so the best plan is to sow in early spring and then leave the pots for a year or so where the weather can get at them but in shade and protected from vermin. Either extracted seed or whole dried berries may be sown.

Yucca species
Woody members of
the lily family,
medium-sized

Yuccas germinate well from spring sowings with bottom heat. Soaking in water for 24 hours may improve germination rates, as the seeds are somewhat hard-coated.

15

SOME TRICKY PERENNIALS AND BULBS

Aconitum MONKSHOOD	Dormancy: sow in autumn outside or chill for 40 days before sowing in spring.
Actaea BANEBERRY	Dormancy: as above. Berries are poisonous.
Alstroemeria PERUVIAN LILY	Dormancy: hard seed coat. Soak for 24 hours. Sow in individual pots. Requires warmth then cold: sow in heat when ripe, then chill for 21 days, then return to heat. Process works in spring as well.
Anemone WINDFLOWER	Dormancy: Sow in autumn outside or chill for 40 days before sowing in spring.
Anemonopsis acrophylla	Lime-hater. Sow in spring in lime-free compost.
Anthericum liliago ST BERNARD'S LILY	Easy from seed but transplant the bulbs with care.
Anthyllis	Hard seed coat. Soak overnight in water that starts just below boiling point.
Aquilegia (species only) COLUMBINE	Dormancy: Sow in autumn or chill for 20 days before spring sowing.

Armeria THRIFT	Hard seed coat. Soak overnight in water that starts just below boiling point.
Astilbe	Requires light and high humidity. Sow on surface, do not cover with compost. Wrap in clingfilm or polybag until the first seedlings emerge. Treat for damping-off.
Astrantia MASTERWORT	Dormancy. Sow in autumn outside or chill for 35 days before spring sowing.
Baptisia australis FALSE INDIGO	Hard seed coat. Chip or abrade between sheets of sandpaper, then soak in water for 24 hours.
Bergenia	Dormancy. Sow in autumn or not at all.
Clintonia	Lime-hater. Sow in peat-based, lime-free compost.
Codonopsis	Not a lime-hater but germinates badly in a limey compost, so treat as for *Clintonia*.
Colchicum AUTUMN CROCUS	All are easy from seed but *must* be sown as soon soon as ripe.
Convallaria majalis LILY OF THE VALLEY	Double dormancy. Treat as for *Smilacina*.
Crocus species	Easy from seed if sown as soon as ripe. Germination is reduced by storage.
Cyananthus	Small seeds. Do not cover with compost.
Cyclamen species	Sow while still sticky from the pod, otherwise the seeds go profoundly dormant. Never allow the pots to dry out. Transplant after two years. Bought seed should be sown and put into a frame for what is likely to be a period of two years or more.

Cyclamen species	Alternatively, the following may be tried: place moist kitchen paper in the inverted lid from a jar of coffee. Place the seeds on the paper. Wrap the whole in clingfilm and cover with a piece of hardboard to keep out the light. Place this on a warm but not sunny windowsill. Inspect this every week until germination begins and then prick off each seed as it germinates.
Cypripedium LADY'S SLIPPER	Hardy orchid. Don't bother: needs laboratory treatment.
Dicentra	Dormancy. Sow in autumn or chill for 21 days before spring sowing.
Disporum FAIRY BELLS	Dormancy: lime-hater. Sow in peaty compost in autumn or chill for 30 days before spring sowing. The best results are obtained by sowing in heat at about 15.5°C (60°F).
Eccremocarpus CHILEAN GLORY FLOWER	Requires light. Do not cover with compost.
Eryngium SEA HOLLY	Dormancy. Sow in autumn or chill for 21 days before spring sowing. Sometimes results are acceptable without chilling.
Erythronium	Easy from seed sown when ripe but difficult to germinate thereafter and may take another one or even two years.
Euphorbia (cold-country species only)	Dormancy: resistant seed coat. Sow in autumn or chill for 14 days before spring sowing. Soak in water for half a day before sowing. Warm temperate species: sow in spring, no chilling, no soaking necessary.
Foeniculum FENNEL	Intolerant of root damage. Sow where it is to grow, then thin.

Freesia

Some of the varieties of this most fragrant of flowers germinate at around 18°C (65°F). They should be chipped with a knife like sweet peas, as the coats are hard and impermeable (see page 36). Sow thinly in deep pots. Plants will need daily watering: dryness is fatal. Do not alow them to fall below 7°C (45°F) or flowers will not be formed. Successional sowings give staggered flowering. Ventilate well.

Gentiana **(European)** GENTIAN

Dormancy; intolerant of root damage. Sow in autumn or chill for 80 days before spring sowing. Take extreme care when pricking out.

Gentiana **(Asiatic)** GENTIAN

Dormancy; lime-haters. As above but lime-free compost.

Geranium CRANESBILL

Seed-coat inhibitors: dormant embryo. Sow in autumn. Chilling for 24 days may produce limited germination in spring. Occasionally there is an atypical massive germination from untreated spring sowings.

Glaucium HORNED POPPY

Tap-rooted. Sow where they are to grow. Subsequently, allow to self-seed and then thin.

Gunnera

Light-induced dormancy. Sow on peaty compost, do not cover the seeds. Keep dark but not entirely so – *some* light is necessary but bright daylight has instant 'trigger' effect. Temperature 15°C (60°F).

Helleborus CHRISTMAS ROSE; LENTEN ROSE

Dormancy. Sow in autumn outside and be prepared to wait. Some people are skin-sensitive to seeds.

Hemerocallis DAY LILY

Partial dormancy. Sow outside in autumn. Spring sowings give reasonable results without chilling, but a 30-day chill doubles the germination rate.

Helleborus

Iris

Sedum

Eryngium

Some of our best
known herbaceous
plants are notoriously
difficult to germinate
because of dormancy,
but can be treated in
several ways to over-
come it. Sow species
only, not garden
varieties (cultivars)

Incarvillea	Require heat. Sow in autumn outside or in spring at 18°C (65°F). Germination can take two months or even more.
Iris	Dormancy. Sow all types in autumn outdoors. May take from four months to two or even three years.
Lathyrus SWEET PEA; EVERLASTING PEA	Hard seed coat. Sow annual sweet peas in autumn in cold frame, overwintering the seedlings in it or sow in spring where the plants are to grow. Sow perennials in spring in cold frame. Soak all seeds in water for 12 hours before sowing or chip the seed coats. The latter is preferable, as *lathyrus* seeds can become waterlogged and die.
Libertia	Require light. Sow in autumn broadcast or in spring in pots indoors without covering the compost.
Lupinus LUPIN	Hard seed coat. Sow annuals in spring or early autumn where they are to flower. Perennials in spring in cold frame. Chip seeds, abrade with sandpaper (see p.37) or soak. This is not necessary with the shrubby *Lupinus arboreus,* the so-called tree lupin, which probably germinates faster than of any ornamental plant, often fully germinated 24 hours after sowing. Rare forms of lupins can be pre-germinated on moist blotting paper and then carefully potted individually.
Lychnis CAMPION	Impermeable seed coat. Dormancy. Sow in autumn or chill for 14 days before abrading or soaking before spring sowing.
Meconopsis BLUE POPPY	Require light. *Meconopsis* are said to be difficult but are not really. Split the batch if you have doubts, sowing half in autumn and half in early spring with bottom heat. You could have

Meconopsis	difficulty overwintering the tiny seedlings from the autumn sowing. Over-winter storage systems must be particularly good if you are going to sow in spring, otherwise the results may be disappointing. Contrary to current belief, viability is not lost by springtime in cool, dry conditions. Sow on a lime-free, peaty compost and do not cover the seed.
Nerine bowdenii	Sow the fleshy seeds immediately the pods split and do not cover the seeds. Germination is extremely fast.
Nomocharis	Beautiful lily-relatives that germinate easily but loathe root disturbance. Sow two or three seeds in each individual pot and plant the whole potful after two years.
Papaver orientale ORIENTAL POPPY	Requires light. Do not cover with compost.
Penstemon **(herbaceous)**	I have never encountered the expected problems with dormancy. Contrary to the shrubby penstemons, which need cool conditions, the perennials appreciate bottom heat at about 15°C (60°F) when sown in early spring.
Polygonatum SOLOMON'S SEAL	Dormancy. Sow in autumn in a frame or chill for 21 days before spring sowing.
Primula	Low viability: require light. I have never experienced the least difficulty with seed of primulas provided that the seed has been fresh or stored cold. Do not cover with compost.
Pulsatilla	Dormancy, low viability of some seeds, dormancy in others. Sow in autumn, nose down, tail in air. The seed will twist itself into the compost. Spring sowing; chill for 21 days then sow with the tails removed.

Ranunculus	Profound dormancy develops. Sow in a frame out of doors. The whole family Ranunculaceae is a problem and all are best sown in autumn. Spring sowing after a 28-day chill may result in germination in two years – or seedlings may never emerge at all.
Roscoea	Dormancy. Sow in autumn outside or chill for 21 days before spring sowing.
Sedum STONECROP	As for *Roscoea*.
Smilacina FALSE SOLOMON'S SEAL	Double dormancy. Chill for 90 days, then put in warmth for 90 days, chill again for 90 days, then bring into warmth for germination. Propagate by division if you possibly can.
Trillium WOOD LILY	Exactly the same as *Smilacina,* with patience, a peaty compost and consistent moisture.
Trollius GLOBEFLOWER	Dormancy. Sow in autumn or chill for 21 days before spring sowing.
Tulipa TULIP	Sow as soon as ripe but be prepared for up to five years to pass before flowering.

INDEX

INDEX